THE LATE
AMERICAN
NOVEL

THE LATE AMERICAN NOVEL

WRITERS ON THE FUTURE OF BOOKS

EDITED BY

Jeff Martin &
C. Max Magee

Soft Skull Press | Berkeley
AN IMPRINT OF COUNTERPOINT

Library of Congress Cataloging-in-Publication Data
The late American novel : writers on the future of books / edited by Jeff Martin and C. Max Magee ; with an introduction by Jeff Martin and C. Max Magee.
    p. cm.
Includes bibliographical references and index.
ISBN-13: 978-1-59376-404-3
ISBN-10: 1-59376-404-9
  1. Books and reading—Forecasting. 2. Books—Forecasting. 3. Authorship—Forecasting. 4. Literature—Appreciation—United States—Forecasting. I. Martin, Jeff, 1980- II. Magee, C. Max. III. Title.

Z1003.L35 2011
002.01'12—dc22

     2010035658

Cover image by Thomas Allen
Cover design by Sharon McGill
Interior design by Neuwirth & Associates, Inc.
Printed in the United States of America

Soft Skull Press
An Imprint of Counterpoint LLC
1919 Fifth Street
Berkeley, CA 94710

www.softskull.com
www.counterpointpress.com

Distributed by Publishers Group West

10 9 8 7 6 5 4 3 2 1

"It doesn't matter how good or bad the product is, the fact is that people don't read anymore."

—Steve Jobs

"If serious reading dwindles to near nothingness, it will probably mean that the thing we're talking about when we use the word 'identity' has reached an end."

—Don DeLillo

"With my eyes closed, I would touch a familiar book and draw its fragrance deep inside me. This was enough to make me happy."

—Haruki Murakami

CONTENTS

Contents

INTRODUCTION

Jeff Martin and C. Max Magee

F. Scott Fitzgerald famously remarked, "There are no second acts in American lives." While true in his specific case and dramatic in that Lost Generation sort of way, this statement has been proven wrong time and again. From Richard Nixon to John Travolta, American life is filled to the brim with second acts. Some lucky people even manage a third or fourth (Cher, anyone?). But this phenomenon isn't limited to people; we see it all around us. The LP was declared dead years ago, yet more and more bands are putting new material out on vinyl. The Boomers are dusting off their old turntables and their grandkids are buying new ones. What's out of fashion becomes *retro*, then goes *vintage*, and then comes back into fashion again. It all comes down to one word: reinvention. The word itself conjures up images as evocative of the stereotypical American dream as apple pie, Aaron Copland, or Chevrolet. In America, you can arrive a pauper and leave a prince, or at the very least own a home with a low interest rate and a TV that gets 300 channels. It's been called the "Land of

Opportunity" for quite some time, but a more apt description would be the "Land of Reinvention."

Our media consumption over the past century or so looks like a Darwinian chart, a rapid evolution from gears and cranks to miniaturized Space Age sleekness. In that short time we've gone from phonographs to iPods, from 16mm reels of film to Blu-ray discs. But in that time, one format has remained virtually unchanged until recently: the book.

The written word's last big format change turned out to be a pretty big deal, fomenting revolutions and laying the groundwork for modern civil society, the scientific revolution, and modernity itself. Gutenberg's big coup sent shockwaves through palace halls across Europe (though, it should be noted, moveable type printing had been invented earlier in Asia) and soon reverberated around the globe. With the invention of the bound, printed, mass-produced book, medieval scribes found themselves left with an obsolete skill set. Latin and Greek faded as the *linguae francae* of the learned classes when printers sprang up and produced books in the local vernacular. Never before had shared knowledge been so accessible to so many. So alien and threatening to the established monopolies of knowledge, power, and morality were these insidious new devices that they set off a struggle that has raged on and on and on, from early sixteenth-century France, when King Francis I briefly made book printing a capital offence—His Royal Highness reacting to the new technology's facility for inciting religious schism—to the book-banning brigades picketing your local library today.

The proliferation of printed books also led to developments like the standardized spelling of the words you'll read in these pages—because who cared about spelling previously, when reading was a rarity?—and a greater awareness of the rules of grammar, which are nearly impossible to codify without a visual and intellectual understanding of language. The impact of the mechanical reproduction of books, though it did not register as lightning fast as the technological change of today, was nothing short of the remaking of civilization. And even as other media have followed the book and usurped its position at the center of cultural exchange, it still seems vital for us as a species to consider what a change in the essential form of the book might mean for our future.

Because into this heady mix has come something as new and potentially paradigm-shifting as those first German Bibles. With the advent of e-readers, near infinite data storage capability, and a shift to a more sustainable and digitized culture, a sea change is upon us. Will books survive? And in what form? Can you really say you're reading a book without holding one in your hands? These and other similar questions have shaped this collection.

We don't claim to know what will happen to the traditional bound and printed book, but there's no shortage of discussion about the road that lies ahead. We wanted to hear from some of today's most promising literary voices, to find out if they are optimistic, apathetic, or just scared shitless. And as might be expected, there is no general consensus. Some of the writers included in this anthology have devised ingenious schemes and strategies, seeking to mark out future spaces in which books will survive and even thrive. Others expect future generations to encounter dystopian literary landscapes, where the merging of media and digital technology leaves books unrecognizable and somehow diminished in the eyes of readers. Some offer confident prognostications about literature's future in this increasingly digital age, while others candidly admit they have no idea what lies ahead.

So if you're reading these words on a device that requires batteries, charge it up before you get too deep. If you're staring at a dog-eared paperback, now's the time to get yourself a cup of coffee.

Here we go.

THE FUTURE OF PAPER

Rivka Galchen

The avian flu morphs yet again. (Those flu viruses are so adept at evolving.) The pigs had the flu, as did the chickens, the Canadians, the zebra mussels, the horseshoe crabs, maybe even the honeybees (we still don't know as the paperwork hasn't been filed yet). Then the flu spread from live cranes to folded paper cranes, and from there to Laffy Taffy wrappers (some argue that the flu hit the candy wrappers before the cranes, that there was a mix-up in paper/crane taxonomy), and then back to the paper cranes more virulently. But somehow no one was too worried, not then; maybe everyone was even secretly pleased because paper cranes have long seemed hackneyed and sentimental... From there the virus morphed to infect broadsheets and then pamphlets and then magazines and then books. (Yes, debate exists there too, about the order, about who infected whom, but I for one suspect that the tuberculosis hit all paper at once, that we only learned about the origami and the candy wrappers first because we lived more closely with them than with our books and magazines.)

But once the paper started coughing, sputtering blood, acquiring jaundice, etc ... once that happened—truth be told, we hadn't even liked paper that much before—we realized that, like the passenger pigeon and the woolly mammoth and electric blue, we were going to miss paper when it was gone. The dying look so good. Doc Holliday is a heartthrob. It was good for books to suddenly seem more like Doc Holliday and less like a well-intentioned middle school teacher in a beige vest. We had all been happily neglecting the books; then they became, in their death throes, as Hollywood-compelling, as gala event-able, as, say, AIDS research, or the environment. Which isn't to say we were able to do much, but we sure did document—in digital media— ourselves not doing it.

In Brooklyn, a paper-making collective was formed. A neglected commercial space for the collective was renovated with great flair and through the sweat of women with really cute bangs. However, the original Save Paper mission became overshadowed by the collective's far more successful sideline of selling homemade organic yogurt and handmade patches created by prisoners whose only thread was harvested from striped gym socks.

The Imperiled Pulp campaign increased awareness, though perhaps at a price to the polar bears, who, for a key spell, were forgotten.

And so sad that the vaccines failed! Though young people made pocket money in the clinical trials.

Suddenly chapbooks—fleeting as rice paper in humidity—were all the rage.

The admirable Paper Chase retrospective film festival had a misguided curatorial vision.

And then there was the rematerialization movement. All those ludicrous late letter presses. Rematerialization—that word, I thought at first it must refer to the finding of bodies for ghosts.

Because as for me: I didn't care about paper. I didn't even care about words. I cared about so much, although to the exclusion of so much more. They say there are now more people living than have ever died. It was only insomuch as paper was becoming a legion of ghosts that I could find it in my heart to take an interest in it, accustomed as I'd grown to taking interest exclusively in the gone.

A BOOK IS A PLACE

Joe Meno

A girl was reading *Franny and Zooey*. Or maybe it was *Nine Stories*. The important thing is that the girl was a girl I had fallen badly for, and the book was lying on the floor of her dorm room, and after I had made my intentions known, and she reciprocated, and I reciprocated, and we reciprocated ourselves right out of our clothes, I saw the small white book sitting on the floor and picked it up as she ran off to the bathroom, bare knees buckled together, to wash off the least important part of me. While she was gone, I began reading, and then she returned and began to get dressed and said she had to go class, but asked if I wanted to stay, and I said, all right and so I kept on reading. I read all afternoon in this girl's bed whom I hardly knew, turning the pages, enjoying the sour milk smell of the girl's sheets, the glorious perfume of her faint sweat and shampoo and toothpaste. And there was something about reading that book, in that particular room, at that particular time in my life that made an inimitable impression on my life. When I was finished, it was dark outside and I went out into the dark and wandered around, stumbling, reaching out to touch the leaves on the trees, the petals of flowers, an iron fence, and for the first time in my life, I was struck dumb by a profoundly serious sort of wonder, which, in the end, is the exact same thing as falling in love.

And there have been other moments like that one: in airports and bus stations and various waiting rooms, clinics, at the DMV, on buses or subway cars or the backseats of vehicles, or in many different beds, or once in a motel room tub, reading a copy of Donald Barthleme's *Forty Stories* and having that electric shock of recognition only a great short story can deliver, feeling embarrassed for having never read such a great writer until that moment. Or sitting on the seventh floor of the Harold Washington Public Library as an art student, pretending to read *Naked Lunch*, hating it, hoping someone, anyone would notice and be impressed, or in a hospital room, holding my breath, waiting for my daughter to wake up only a few hours after she was born, not wanting to make a noise, too tired, too excited to sleep, watching her lying there— swaddled tight, pink cap atop her head—and flipping through a book entitled *Breastfeeding: A Guide*, searching among the pages for some clue, some answer, something to keep me from feeling like I was only pretending to be a father now. *X-Men #112*, which my typically stoic father bought for me during a rough bout of strep throat, which I read in a fort I had built of pillows and sheets in our mold-smelling basement, and the fact that my father bought it for me made me wonder if maybe I was dying, and being seven or eight years old and having never read a comic book before, I paged through it carefully, ignoring my cough, trying to understand what was happening, feeling like some other world had suddenly revealed itself to me.

There are so many more moments, and although all these books have touched me in similar ways since, what I've come to acknowledge or slowly accept is that the idea of the book is more important than the actual form it takes—the message, the content being more vital than the medium—and that throughout the history of narrative arts, storytelling has always adapted to these changing forms and technologies, and has managed to not only survive, but begin anew each time, introducing a whole other generation to the possibilities of reading. The Kindle, the iPad, these are just variations of a need we have as a civilization, as a species, to use our imagination, and this need is as important in this time as any other.

For me, a book, in whatever form it takes—hardbound copy, paperback, electronic version, online instrument, text downloaded on a cell phone, even a story read orally—a book is actually a place, a place where we, as adults, still have the chance to engage in active imagining, translating word to image, connecting these images to memories, dreams, and larger ideas. Television, film, even the stage play, have already been imagined for us, but the book, in whatever form we choose to interact with it, forces us to complete it. Television, film, and stage plays do not need us; they exist in completion whether we interact with them or not. But a book, a novel, a short story, even a comic book, needs us to complete the action, to see using our mind's eye, which gets less use the older we get, the farther we step from childhood games of make-believe. The fact that books provide us the place to imagine is critically important, as it is there, in the imagination, that all sense of possibility rests. The idea of books—what is a book, and what isn't—is one of the most interesting questions in the world to me, because there isn't an answer, and by simply trying to find one, an entire world of imaginative possibilities reveals itself to us.

THE FUTURE OF WRITING IS IN MY JACKET

Michael Paul Mason

If you want to know where writing is going, you shouldn't look in a library or a bookstore. You shouldn't even look online. Instead, you should rummage through the pockets of your nearest writer for clues. Take a peek in that writer's book bag, purse, or backpack. You'll find everything you need to know.

In the right inside pocket of my jacket, where most people might carry sunglasses, you'll find a Panasonic LX3 camera. It has a Leica lens capable of switching to wide-angle shots, and I can use the camera to shoot video as well. In the left inside pocket, I have an Olympus LS-11 voice recorder. The camera and the recorder are more important to me than pen and paper. And while my jacket functions as a portable production studio, it's my satchel that does (and requires) the heavy lifting. My satchel is a worn-out leather bag, once a rich amber color, now frayed and graying like myself. I take it everywhere I go, and when the weather's too warm for wearing my jacket, the satchel ends up carrying the camera and recorder for me. In any season, though, you'll find it packed with all sorts of nerdtastic goodies. Right now, it contains a neoprene laptop sleeve (where I keep the laptop I used to type this essay), three pens and a highlighter, a Moleskine notebook that I use for writing notes to my daughters when I travel, a laptop charger, a portable hard drive, two video adapter cables, an ethernet cord, business cards, a pair of German-made, surgeon-grade nail clippers (I obsessively cut my nails to the quick), an LED flashlight keychain, a paperback book, a folder pocket full of release forms, and several transcripts of interviews I've conducted (for the book I'm working on, I email my audio files to a transcriber). Although I carry pens and paper in my satchel, I don't use them much other than for quick note-taking—phone numbers, memos, grocery lists. I haven't outsourced those tasks to my phone. Yet.

I'm a writer, and yet I acknowledge that the tools of my trade have more in common with those used by a Hollywood director than a typist. Yes, I still deal with words, but the words are complemented by the sounds and images I record while doing my work. When I conduct interviews, I always record rather than take notes. It isn't that I don't trust note-taking; it's that I might also turn that interview into source material for a radio production (which, I might add, requires its own kind of writing). I also take pictures when I'm conducting interviews, because they help me remember details I might otherwise forget: the goofy collared shirt my subject wore, the little boy doing a puzzle in the corner of the patio, the manufacturer's name on a piece of lab equipment. As a result of carrying these tools, I've learned to use them. I can edit audio, I can Photoshop pictures, and I can cobble together video. I don't consider myself a photographer, a radio professional, or a director, but nobody expects that of me. They expect me to write, and they're curious about the places and people I visit.

When I finish writing my current book, I expect to have dozens of hours of audio and video from the interviews I conducted. I'll probably have hundreds of photos. I plan to take the best moments from all those interviews and use them for the book. But then I'll take those same moments, and perhaps others, and use them to enhance the book, in the same way that a person can enhance the experience of a movie by listening to a director's commentary or watching a "making of" special feature. Writing, for me, has become a production beyond sentences and paragraphs.

Readers who are interested in my writings might go to my website and see photos and videos I've posted about my travels and my work. Just recently, I posted a video of a set of perfused pig lungs breathing independently of a body, under a glass dome. The video only lasted several seconds, but it drew a great number of comments online. Readers were intrigued and wanted to know more about my project, and that's a good thing for a writer. Like anybody else, we want people to take an interest in our work, but historically, writers have always let publishers drum up that interest. You might call this endeavor marketing or self-promotion, but that's an ugly word that implies a purely profit-driven motive. I don't think all the photography and audio and video recordings are going to sell more books, necessarily. I'm doing those things because I enjoy doing them, and I like sharing things with my readers. If it ends up selling more books, then great, but if not, at least I have a wonderful archive, a sort of multimedia documentary, of the work I've done. This approach to writing—one of sharing and connecting—has usurped the traditionally hip notion of writer-as-recluse. Today, readers perceive an unattractive, neurotic quality in writers who hide or distance themselves from their audience.

As for me, I enjoy connecting. It doesn't take much effort on my part to write a few sentences on my blog, send a message to my audience, or post a link to the newest article on brain research. I don't feel the need to do it every day, but I think connecting with readers sends them a message that helps dispel a lot of terrible stereotypes about writers. We're not prima donnas; we work hard. We don't sit around and wait for inspiration; we're constantly looking for storytelling opportunities. In fact, this year, I've written three different articles based on stories I've found with the help of my friends and fans on Facebook. It's an anthropological goldmine, if that sort of writing intrigues you.

So, you take a peek in my pockets, and you think that perhaps I'm correct, and that maybe writing is going digital and that a writer needs to learn how to work a camera and a microphone. But I'd say that's just the surface, and that something far stranger is happening. I think the traditional roles of artists are eroding, that the lines distinguishing filmmakers and visual artists and musicians and writers are fading so that any single person can effectively pull off a serious project in any medium. Tomorrow's writers will be illustrating their own book covers, publishing coffee table books of photos to accompany their bestsellers, self-broadcasting their interviews to public radio stations, running their own video channels online, and releasing films they've adapted from their own work. And they'll be doing this with the help of publishers. As the technology gets easier to operate, more and more voices will chime in, but it will be the writers, chief among the other artists, who stand to succeed the most. At the heart of their craft is storytelling, and it will be story—in the most classical sense of the word—that achieves relevance in our wondrous, imploding world.

I MISS BOOKS LIKE I MISS MY BICYCLE (OR, RIDING A HORSE WITH HAY FEVER)

Clancy Martin

After the end of books I felt a sense of relief. It was how the new clergy felt under Martin Luther when they realized that Latin lessons were going to be two hours shorter. When I was six years old, my brother gave me *Papillon* to read and I waded through the 576-page autobiography—my favorite scene was when the leper throws his finger into the fire—thinking that it was a reasonable book for me to digest. True, I was an ambitious reader. I disdained to enter the library book-reading contests because they were just for kids. It was my plan to read only what adults would enjoy. I hid my *Conans*, my Heinlein, and my Burroughs "Mars" paperbacks; Jules Verne I thought was permissible because he was translated from French. Somehow I thought that Edgar Allan Poe was also a kids' writer so I hid his stories, too. My mother read Stephen King and Erma Bombeck so I read all of those; I don't remember what else she read, but anything she kept by her bed stand I took to my room and ate it up before she returned it to the library. Many of them I enjoyed, of course; most of everything I read I relished; and when I conceived the project, at age fifteen or sixteen, of reading everything in the Western canon, beginning with *The Odyssey*, I discovered what all readers of the great books realize: they are not the sluggish monsters we expected but the very most enjoyable books to read, the easiest books, the fastest, the "beach reads." (Literature hiccupped in the twentieth century and produced a few exceptions to this rule: *Finnegan's Wake*, *The Making of Americans*, a few others I'm not thinking about, because they were painful. But even Thomas Mann's massive *Joseph and His Brothers*—written by a master whose books nevertheless are, as a rule, a bit clayfooted—reads almost breathlessly. But the truth is, all this time I was reading both for pleasure and as a duty. It was as though I was counting the books as I went. Students would enter my office, later, and ask, "Have you really read all these books?" (a student's all-time favorite kiss-ass office question), and I could say, "All but that one and the other beside it, and I'm getting to those next week," or something like that. There was a time, a long time, when I wouldn't put a book on my shelf unless I had read it.

Then, hallelujah, they decided to stop books. At first I was annoyed, because in the meantime I had begun writing them, and even counting on the little bit of income involved. Thank God I hadn't quit, as they say, my day job. My day job—I'm a professor—involved books in theory but very little in practice. It was more an exercise in pretending about books. The students pretended to have read the books and I pretended to have something illuminating to say about them. I pretended to be an expert in the books—books that I had in many cases read only once, and a long time ago, or sometimes only a handful of paragraphs in, or someone else's synopsis of, or even not at all. In this way class was a bit like a literary party or barroom conversation where we discussed the latest books that we hadn't read but pretended we had or had begun to, and about which we all had strong opinions, but were equally and agreeably circumspect about avoiding mention of characters, events, and plot twists. So, professor-wise, the end of books was a painless solution to an "Emperor's New Clothes" scenario that I felt was otherwise bound to result in my humiliation sooner or later, as I was, after all, the emperor in question, even though I had become very deft at deferring pointed questions from the occasional student who had done the reading to hapless innocents among the class. "Aha! Someone hasn't done their reading! Well, class, let's work on this one together, shall we?" Then you start with the woman who asked the question in the first place. "And what do you think? Give us a little background." We've all been to college, we know the routine. So, yes, no more whited sepulcher at the chalkboard, that was a good thing.

Initially we switched to blogs, which were free, short, usually had nice pictures—I don't like the long ones absent visual aids, myself; they drag on—and we could read them in "real time," right there in the classroom, as a kind of beehive of knowledge, collectively shooting links to one another and twittering like a flock of finches and . . . you get the picture. No syllabus! (Not even online). We had a webpage and every class was like a new day, fresh reading, unexpected suggestions, sites to discover. It was very contemporary, everything as shiny as a new pair of shoes, with that glossy magazine effect but without those annoying little cards falling out every time you open it. Blogs led us to video games, and if you want to talk about the mind-body problem or Heidegger's notion of angst, frankly, you could do a lot worse than *Red Dead Redemption*. Plus, you don't think these things are going to be fun until you try them—then, I'm telling you, watch out. I spend hours preparing for class now, at home in the basement, whereas I used to squeeze in twenty minutes in my office between emails before filling my coffee cup and walking into the lecture hall.

That moaning from the poets. Back in the old days, did you ever actually try to suffer through an afternoon with a poet, a real live practicing poet? There's a reason we all stayed drunk back then. I hope my three daughters will be programmers. It was poets who killed the books, if we want to tell the truth about it. Take this top-forty number: "The apparition of these faces in the crowd; / Petals on a wet, black bough." Now, really. Right up there with things depending on red wheelbarrows in the rain. I mean, what are you supposed to *do* with that? It's an honest question. You might as well try to squeeze the juice from Heraclitus. And I'll admit it, "In a Station of the Metro" used to be a favorite of mine! All sarcasm aside, when this is the finest fruit of our most celebrated writers, I'm with the book-killers. But, like many of us, I was buying into this complex Persian-carpet-fraud that took centuries to weave and was a masterpiece of the Middle Ages and the Renaissance and yet took all of three or four people, say Al Gore, Bill Gates, Jeff Bezos, and Steve Jobs, a handful of years to unravel.

Now I miss books as much as I miss my bicycle. There was a time I would have ridden a horse to work (and a miserable time it would have been, too, as I have hay fever). Now if I want to read, voila, I touch a button: pictures-text-video-music, it's better than the movie version of *Where the Wild Things Are* (well, much better). Instead of some dead pedant blowing wind, I can interact with other creative minds *as they create*, unedited, the raw stuff, but also with the high bar of capitalism to Folsom flop: because we won't view it if it ain't what the market will view. Count your hits. That's the new paradigm, folks: *viewing*, not reading. Hell, non-human animals don't read, but they view, and they seem a whole lot happier than we do (at least, when they're not in captivity). *Aesthesis* in the old-fashioned sense. Like Plato said: "the lovers of sights and sounds"! And our new native environment is virtual. Even when we had books, I spent more time returning emails than

I did reading. Reading books, I mean. Maybe an hour at night before falling asleep, my wife (twelve years younger) surfing the web beside me, a warped-covered, heavy-papered, coffee-stained *Swann's Way* or *The Idiot* resting on my chest. Truth is I read my computer screen and my iPhone all day long. Or viewed them, I should say. Caught me backsliding there. And I don't feel guilty any more! There's no end to what one might read, so a plan like I once had of holding the canon in my head is like planning to swim across the Pacific; why not rather have fun simply splashing in the waves? It's called *surfing* the web. You stay on the surface. When you're under the wave, it's because you've fallen off the board.

As for being freed from the obligation to write books, well, enough said.

NOT QUITE AS DIRE
AS HAVING YOUR SPINE RIPPED
OUT, BUT . . .

Owen King

At one time or another pretty much every male of my generation endured the special embarrassment of having to sit by while an adult attempted to learn how to play a video game. I can specifically recall my friend's dad, Mr. Winter, coming downstairs to their finished basement—nicely kitted out with a Ping-Pong table, a pool table, and posters of Larry Bird—to find a gang of us huddled on our knees around a Nintendo, like little worshipers. Probably Mr. Winter wanted to make sure we weren't tearing up the felt on his pool table trying to do trick shots, or maybe he was worried we might be smoking pot. All we were doing, though, was playing *Mortal Kombat*.

Mortal Kombat was the preeminent fight game of my early-'90s adolescence, a side-scrolling, hand-to-hand battle between two bristling warriors. The goal was simple: to direct your avatar through a series of kicks, jabs, and "special moves" until your opponent was battered into submission, and stood before you, wobbling and utterly vulnerable. Then, if you knew the right combination of buttons, you could perform a "fatality." Depending on the character you were inhabiting, this might mean you beheaded your prey, or kicked a hole through him, or something along those lines. Most famously, if your avatar was the vicious Sub-Zero, you could top off a victory in the traditional manner—by tearing out your opponent's spine.

Mr. Winter's reaction to whatever "fatality" he saw was something along the lines of "Ouch," or "Oh, wow." He was one of the cool dads, relaxed about the grab-assing that was a part of any get-together among boys of our age, and easy with pizza money. Still, he must have been a bit rattled by our facility for murder.

"So—what—you're just supposed to kill the other guy?" he asked.

No. You're supposed to hug him.

Yes, you're supposed to fucking kill him! You're supposed to extract his cowardly spine from his body and hold it up in the air for him to see, so that as he goes spiraling down to the depths of hell, he'll carry the knowledge that you have taken possession of his most vital organ, that you may very well be tickling it, or licking it, or using it as a pretend pony and cantering around with it between your legs like a complete lunatic, while he is dancing on hot coals for eternity! What could be more obvious than that?

To his credit, Mr. Winter tried to play it cool; he asked to have a turn. Since in all likelihood he had paid for the game, and there was the little matter of it being his house, we couldn't refuse. He was a fish in a barrel, of course, because no fifteen-minute tutorial in the utility of the different buttons could mitigate the ass-kicking that lay in store for him.

Not that everyone wasn't perfectly nice about it. There was none of the showboating or boasting that went along with normal battles. It was too sad a spectacle.

In the end, there was Mr. Winter, an adult—a grown person with a job, with a driver's license, a man who had had sex—

thumbing buttons like crazy, to no perceivable effect while his character was hurled around and repeatedly stepped on by the avatar of a thirteen-year-old zit-popper (yours truly) who manipulated his controller as effortlessly as a stenographer and with the same divorced expression. When it was over, I'm pretty sure Mr. Winter just laughed and handed back the controller, said thanks for the lesson, and went upstairs—perhaps to sit on the couch and drink a cold one in the bright and peaceful quiet of his living room.

He was an adult, after all, and it was just a game. It wasn't like his real spine had been ripped out.

E-readers and e-books feel as foreign to me as I imagine *Mortal Kombat* did to Rick's dad. I find them flabbergasting. More than that, I find them slightly alarming. I won't be so melodramatic as to claim that the new technology makes me feel as though someone is rummaging around in my thorax, but it doesn't fill me with delight.

To begin with, after repeated efforts, I still find it difficult to read fiction—even my own—on a screen. Print on the screen tends to speed up my eye; my eye wants to slide. When I edit a document, I greatly prefer to do so on paper, because it takes longer for me to handwrite than it does for me to type, and I believe that this forces me to be more thoughtful about word choices, sentence construction, and so on.

This aversion is almost certainly a consequence of long-held habit or personal idiosyncrasy. I'm probably not trying hard enough. I don't mean to be a Luddite, and I'm speaking entirely for myself. I belong to the tail-end of the last generation whose first computer was an electric typewriter and who didn't know that email existed until college. On some level, I'm still coming to grips with the Roomba. It could very well be that my inner fogey is just squawking over one technological advance too many. I should be happier for the trees.

That said, I don't believe it's unreasonable to have some concern about "the future of the book" in the context of a world where more immediate diversions—music, movies, video games—are all readily available in the same portable device. While novels have been in competition with these entertainments for years, and it hasn't stopped a diverse audience of readers from flocking to Jonathan Franzen and John Grisham alike, the difference now is that for many people, their books will be snuggled right up next to the other stuff on their iPads, or whatever their multimedia machine of choice happens to be. While it's sort of exciting in the abstract to imagine Jonathan Franzen rubbing shoulders in a tight electronic space with your favorite Beck songs, a few choice episodes of *The Wire*, and *ZombieSmash*,* in reality that's an awful lot of potential distraction when you're in the trenches of the difficult first hundred or so pages of *The Corrections*. Again, these temptations are nothing new, but in the past, a person generally needed to at least stand up and take a few steps to get at them.

I still don't expect the book as an object, or the art form of the novel, to disappear any time soon. Future generations may have better attention spans than I give them credit for, and even if they don't, the novel's capacity for seeing more deeply into a character, and for just seeing more—of a place and of a time—than any other medium can permit, is a point of singular appeal that should always have its constituents.

A passage from Joshua Ferris's *The Unnamed*, a moving and

---

* A popular game for the iPhone that I am confident is a lot of fun, and which definitely has its loyalties in order with respect to the war between humanity and the soulless undead.

original novel about the extraordinary transformations that per-verse affliction forces on ordinary people, seems apt:

> He strained to recall a single exchange—on the street, from the next table over at a restaurant—overheard in all the years he had lived in the city, within the inescapable nexus of babble he had sat in most of his life, and not one came to mind. Not one. Had he never unplugged his ears of the self-involvement that consumed him about work, when he wasn't sick, or about sickness, when he couldn't work? Had he never listened?

This is a perspective you could only find in a novel. The thought comes to the reader in a whisper, but in the absence of other noise—all those eager bits and bytes clamoring from inside the small black rectangle in your pocket—it grows loud. No actor could express the same ideas as fully or as persuasively. The only voice you hear is your own.

THE THREE-DAY WEEKEND PLAN

John Brandon

Being a fellow who indulges in nostalgia to an embarrassing degree, a fellow who drinks to mute his *good* memories, I'm prone to consider Golden Ages. Do they exist? Let's be fun-loving and assume they do. Who gets to say when? Anyone who's interested. So, me. Can we be aware of a Golden Age while it's going on? Besides cartoons for thirty-year-olds, what are we in the Golden Age of presently? Once a Golden Age has passed, as it usually has, what then? Should we be ashamed to speak of Golden Ages? If young, ought we be toiling at the creation of Golden Ages, rather than lamenting their passage?

I was in Holland at a literature and music festival and I attended a panel where some guys from McSweeney's sat alongside two Dutch men. One of the Dutch took a populist approach—journals, websites, self-publishing—and he dressed with much texture, wore comfortable shoes, was mildly and evenly disappointed in the world. The other man's hair was held rakishly out of place with some stiffening agent and his suit had a sheen. He was high up in a publishing company. The two Dutchmen knew each other and didn't require much prompting to begin arguing, expertly digging one another without being rude. The sandaled man pointed out that the other's press had founded a glossy culture magazine for no other reason than to publish their own authors in it, promoting those authors' books. He said he read the periodical "in bath," which I took to mean for a moment that he perused it whilst sunk into a tub of bubbles, like the magazine was good for nothing more than mindless relaxation, but later surmised he probably meant he read it while taking a dump, situating the magazine, in the audience's senses, in proximity to evacuated wastes. Either way. The topic arose of why, in Holland, there was nothing like McSweeney's, meaning no well-organized and highly regarded underground literary concern, supported in a limited but fervent manner. The McSweeney's guys had no guess, the sandaled man not much of one. The man in the suit finally said, "Because we do not have need for it." Hmmph. I made that noise, which is not impolite at a panel. I had never questioned the necessity of McSweeney's. In the small picture, their necessity was clear: They published my books. In the large picture, though, their necessity was sort of implied, along with everything else nimble and anti-corporate. Thing was, I hadn't been equipped, growing up in a retirement town in the southern United States, to consider a nation not needing rebellion. Just hadn't occurred to me that one could exist free of embroilment in a culture war—wash your hair and cut your steak and smoke your cigarettes all unaffiliated, no side to be on. I imagined myself this way, tried to, imagined myself as an anarchist after wholesale nuclear chaos, like, *What now?* And I'm sure they enjoy rebellion, the Dutch, at worst in the way frat boys enjoy rap music, at best academically, but the idea had been posited that they didn't need it.

The rest of the trip I paid attention, already growing nostalgic for that land of beer and bracing breezes. I walked the quaint streets, missing them. The pubs were smoke-filled. I ate what they call "fresh" herring, which means *raw* herring. Everyone on a bicycle. I spoke to locals, eating sweaty orange cheese. One thing became obvious—one pertinent thing: These people weren't being told what they liked. There were suggestions being made as to what they might try, but products (for our purposes, entertainment and art products) were not being shoved colorfully and loudly and continually and competitively at them, aggrandized, hyped, over-blurbed, over-displayed. When it came to books, there was an adult atmosphere. Whole bunch of grownups. Now, I don't believe the Dutch are finer folks than Americans. I can't believe that because holding out negligible faith in human nature is key for us nostalgia aficionados. You have to believe everything is being ruined, and it is. You have to believe that any people, given the opportunity, will ruin anything. Any people. Anything. I didn't break new ground in Holland. I came to the simplest conclusion: The population in Holland was too small to warrant the effort it would take to advertise as we do in the States. In the States, one demographic can be singled out—rednecks, teenagers, divorce lawyers—and if ten percent of them are convinced to buy something, it's a windfall. And you can convince them. It's all they know, being told what they like, and that goes equally for letter-jacketed Iowans struggling through community college when they rent action movies as for sharp-spectacled Brooklynites with master's degrees as they stroll into the bookstore. Only we should expect more in the bookstore, if not more from Brooklyn.

So I touched down back in Memphis, the glamour of being flown to Europe worn off, some music akin to Rascal Flatts twanging through the terminal, a sweet roll franchise frowning sweetly as I passed, and I prepared to reenter my life as a low-rent writer of literary fiction. For the purpose of this essay, let's say that was the state I was in. Let's say I was feeling a little sorry for myself. Tiny advances. No foreign rights. No audio rights. No, ha, appearance fees. Let's say I was feeling sad for the end of my trip, sad about my finances, but also sad for the passing of an era, which I couldn't be sure existed, when literary fiction was not just another genre, when it could only be defined by what it was *not*. Did this time exist? Someone tell me. Let's say at that moment it was in my interest to believe that era had indeed existed and had passed, so there'd be a reason I was being ignored. While I located my pickup in a light rain, let's say I was thinking of the '60s and '70s, when, looking back now, it seems writers were allowed to be as odd as they happened to be, and not just one singled-out darling every several years. Was it a better world, or was originality simply a fashion that publishers, at that time, were telling people they wanted? If arriving on the scene today (and if I'm expected to answer this question, it will remain rhetorical), would Joy Williams be allowed to be the exact Joy Williams she is? Would an unknown Padgett Powell, a manuscript for *Edisto* in hand in 2010, be allowed to be the writer Padgett Powell? Those McGuane novels in the Keys? Am I being unwisely specific? Hell, what if Barthelme, as an anonymous youngster, were sending out batches of his stories today, to be read by agents' assistants in New York? I'm probably idealizing the past and I'm certainly whining, but that's what nostalgia-addicted people do. As I mentioned, it's embarrassing.

I know, the future of books. Next let me make a comparison between a place on the Gulf Coast of Florida a couple counties north of Tampa called Citrus County, and the novella. Citrus County is poor, empty of progress and luxury. It's made of bleached white roads and corner stores. Its coastline is a swamp, which means it doesn't possess a beach, you see, and that means few tourists, and that means no resorts, restaurants, shopping malls. It's a rare type of person who intentionally visits Citrus County. The springs and low skies and spindly cattle, they don't do anything other than exist to be looked at. Citrus County has nothing to sell, and therefore remains unmolested. And now look at the novella. Yeah? See? Hold that thought.

Holland. Golden Ages. Advertising. The literature business. Let me take a stab at tying these together before they get away from me completely. I'm nostalgic for the time a couple paragraphs ago, the time before I broke for lunch, when it was enough to muse. So listen. What happened was the comparatively relaxed atmosphere between commerce and the written word in Holland made me realize that in the States, the Golden Age of any fine art form anymore, any literary form, is the age in which the quality of the writing might be greater than the degree to which that writing is in danger of being celebrated and peddled. In other words, the only hope for a Golden Age, anymore, is being ignored. I'm not talking about popular art here. The far aforementioned cartoons for thirty-year-olds are not meant to be ignored and I wouldn't wish that on them. I'm talking about literature. What do you think of at the mention of the "typical contemporary novella," or "mainstream modern novella?" I don't, for one, think of anything. Hmmph. Everything's wide open and equal in novella-land. No complaints being in the ghetto with no manicured suburb to offer contrast. The novella, excepting accidents, is all ghetto. It's Citrus County, if you'll allow me to mix geographical art metaphors, and I think you will. Bluntly, the novella is in its Golden Age as a form *right now* because no one is beating it with a stick until nickels fall out. It had a traditional Golden Age, I'm sure, probably some time in the first half of the twentieth century, or even before that, but now it's having another one, this new kind. The novella, currently, has no use for rebellion. Like Holland, it doesn't need McSweeney's. My plan for the novella is—drum roll: Do nothing. Or do whatever little is required to steward the status quo. Let's agree, shall we, to keep throwing around the inane term Great American Novel, and to never, ever utter the phrase Great American Novella. Let's agree to not remind California what it used to take for granted, that novellas, because of their length, can often be more handily adapted than novels into movies. Let us not remind New York what all the avid and demanding among us take for granted, that a volume of three novellas is more intriguing than one flabby novel. Let us downplay the novella in casual conversation. Writers, if you've a can't-miss commercially viable yarn a-brewing, be good enough to stretch it into a short novel or compress it into a long story. And look, let's keep the novella for ourselves, the adults. We deserve something, don't we? Let's free the novella of prizes and awards and citations and all manner of gold star. Let's fail to educate our students about the novella, fail to convince them of its charms. We need never be nostalgic for the Golden Age of the novella. We've got something they don't want, a non-commodity, and we need to look out for it.

And here is our reward, writers, our chance to steal from the mean universe. Let us each compose a novella, and let us find out, in the writing, how we truly write, and let us revise and question that novella, and let us keep that perfect document hidden in a plain manila envelope until we're surrounded by friends and the weather is fine, over, say, a long weekend at a cabin, and let's each evening before dinner read aloud—thirty pages Friday, say, and thirty Saturday, and bring it all to a head on Sunday afternoon. Can't you hear the ice clinking? The crickets singing? A fox gingerly picking through the foliage? Your own voice, laced with gratitude, warming the porch? You'll be so far from everywhere, and even further. And when you get back home, stash that pile of honestly, fairly spoiled paper up in a musty closet away from any and all publishing apparatus, and if your children can be trusted, if they grow into fine adults as you hope, one day hand it over to them.

GOODBYE TO THE GRAPHOSPHERE

Benjamin Kunkel

For half a millennium, across continents and civilizations, the reading populace did almost nothing but grow and consolidate itself. Steadily, more people in more and more places could read, and could read more books more cheaply, and with increasing ease. Not only were people able to do this, they *chose* to. It would be astonishing to learn, if some retrospective survey could be carried out, that hours per head spent reading *didn't* increase across all capitalist or otherwise modernizing countries (most communist regimes having been energetic promoters of literacy) until at least the middle of the past century.

A few years ago, the French thinker Régis Debray published a brilliant and suggestive essay placing the rise and decline of socialist movements within this frame of ever-greater literacy. The question of socialism can be bracketed for now. More relevant, for the future of reading in general and novel-reading in particular, is Debray's periodization scheme, in which an immemorial *logosphere*—the spoken-word realm of the great religions, whose holy texts had been pronounced by God, transcribed and commented on by a small caste of literate men, and received as gospel by an unlettered general population—was succeeded, starting in 1464, with the invention of Gutenberg's press, by a spreading *graphosphere*, in which an oral relationship to words was supplemented, for mounting numbers of ordinary people, by a literate relationship to them. The demi-millenium of the graphosphere lasted, on Debray's account, until 1968, dawn of the *videosphere*.

The status of 1968 as a watershed no doubt seems more inevitable, less merely convenient, for a Frenchman of Debray's generation than for an American born after the event. Still, the shift he describes is unmistakable. It's not, of course, that inhabitants of the videosphere no longer read, any more than residence in the graphosphere made it impossible to attend the Latin Mass. And the diffusion of radio, decades before TV, had already overlaid the graphosphere with a new kind of electronic orality. So had movie theaters projecting black and white films offered a prewar premonition of the videosphere. But, starting sometime in the first decades after the Second World War, people in the west began to read less (as studies from different countries, including the US, confirm), and what they did read, according to Debray, exercised less sway over them than what they saw in printed or—especially— moving images.

To the logosphere corresponds the dominance of the spoken and heard; to the graphosphere, that of the written and read; and to the videosphere, that of mass-produced audiovisuals received electronically. And Debray aligns other changes with the "mediological" ones. Time itself, once experienced as a circle of eternal repetition, becomes, in the graphosphere, a line of progress charging into the future, before lapsing, in our era, into a series of discrete "presents" distributed around current events. So does the logosphere's central myth of the saint turn into that of the hero—the hero of novels as well as biographies and history books—and the myth of significant *action*, which then gives way, with the videosphere, to a celebrity myth predicated on the apprehension of glamorous *being*. Likewise, the "basis of symbolic authority" is transferred from the invisible (God), to the legible (History), and then to the visible (the Spectacle). The "status of the individual" shifts from subject ("to be commanded") to citizen ("to be persuaded") to consumer ("to be seduced"). History is never as neat as the schemas laid across it, but most people will recognize that Debray's three-act drama has accurately captured its drift.

The English version of his essay—called "Socialism: A Life Cycle"—is based on the French original from 1991. In other words, it doesn't take into account the most significant, not to say contradictory, development for literacy in the years since the demise of the USSR, namely the advancing norm, at least among the global middle class, of what has been called an "always-on" relationship to the multifarious streaming and downloadable content of the internet. This change is not identical with the mass migration online, over dial-up connections, of circa 1994; it arrived only with constant broadband access over portable devices capable of reproducing streaming sounds and images as unerringly as letters and punctuation. Less than a decade ago, it was still almost always easier to open up whatever light and portable paperback book you were in the middle of reading than to avail yourself of any other medium. The only real competition for ease of access was the morning newspaper—already stale by evening—or the Discman, in which you had just the one CD. As for the TV, it restricted you to the living room, and imposed the networks' schedules. Now, with the advent of tablet computing, we contemplate a world in which such activities as watching videos or movies, listening to music, or reading what used to be called "the press" and should now maybe be called "commentary," will for the most part be as convenient, as constantly available, as reading a paperback book once was (and remains). In the contest for our attention, literature previously had rivals in film, TV, radio, and more ephemeral writing; the difference today lies in the availability of all these other things all the time. The playing field, once tilted to the advantage of the cheap and portable book, has been leveled.

The always-on, un-turn-off-able internet obviously enlarges the videosphere. But the internet has also yielded a *digital* graphosphere, as it were, and in this way appears, at first blush, as if it might slow or even reverse an otherwise inexorable eclipse of literary culture. And in a sense, this is the case. Yet while the online universe of texts obviously includes whole books, for purchase or in the public domain, it is dominated by a different kind of writing: news articles, blog posts, op-eds and polemics, short diary entries, updates, announcements, reviews, advertisements, readers' comments, and so on. The most common species of online writing might all be said to belong to the family of "commentary" rather than what is still sometimes called (though not usually without embarrassment) "literature." They have, that is, a sort of secondary status to whatever primary object they comment on; they are prompted by and dependent on some other object or event, whether a commercial product, a recent private experience, a news story, someone else's political opinion, a song or book, or whatever. This is not to disdain commentary for its failure to be primary rather than secondary, only to attempt to suggest its difference from literature. Literature, you might say, transforms the world into an illustration of the text, while commentary's relationship to the world is more like that of a caption to a photograph or a wall-paragraph to a painting.

The news article that formed the germ of *Madame Bovary* might serve as an example of commentary, and Flaubert's novel as one of literature. At the unmarked border between literature and commentary, the regions may be hard to tell apart. But on the whole the climates are distinct for the different natures and longevities of the creatures they support. The would-be piece of literature may not last for decades and generations, but it wants to. The article of commentary may not vanish from everyone's mind after a lifespan measured in days and weeks, but it expects to.

The difference recalls that between *labor* and *work* in Hannah Arendt. *Labor*, as she defines it, flows into goods whose twofold character is to be used up by consumption and to erase the discrete contribution of the individual laborer. *Work*, on the other hand, yields durable objects whose utility is not destroyed by the use of them, and which bear the lasting impress of the individual artisan. Presumably writing will always be more like work, in this sense, than a job as a short-order cook, but if, as Arendt argued, the tendency of the modern world is to establish "a waste economy, in which things must be almost as quickly devoured and discarded as they appear in the world," this process would seem to be overtaking prose along with everything else.

So the internet seems likely to reinforce, rather than overturn, the graphosphere's subordinate relationship to the videosphere, with the role of writing as a whole resembling viewers' comments on YouTube. There are a lot of these comments, some of them very clever, but they're not where the action's at.

This eclipse of the graphosphere by some kind of *digitosphere*— a videosphere combined with a blogosphere—seems to be the context in which to place the future of the novel. In the literary culture of the past few hundred years, novels dominate the landscape like a mountain range, but one that is even more impressive for its massive centrality than for the heights of its summits. Unquestionably some of the towering books of modern times were novels, but other peaks, more isolated but just as high, were thrust up by philosophy, poetry, history, economics, autobiography, psychoanalysis, anthropology, etc. So the eminence of the novel in literary culture owed nothing to any monopoly on greatness. It derived instead from the novel's special status as a popular form, written by and for amateurs rather than scholars, that could nevertheless achieve true artistry, that could be at once "of the best" and "of the (middle-class) people." Familiarity with good or great novels, even if there wasn't so much as a handful of them that everybody had read, connected all literary or educated people into a society of book readers.

The inherent amateurishness of the novel, of its writers and implied readers alike, seems vital in this. Not that no authors relied on writing novels to make a living; obviously many did and do. But (as the fictional novelist Bill Gray remarked in *Mao II*) the novel was essentially a democratic form, and writing one a feat that potentially anybody could pull off at least once. Among the audience, even less expertise or specialization was required. To read a novel you had to be literate and to take an interest in life as it's lived by individuals, and that was about it. The great novelistic subjects—manners, family, growing-up, alienation, friendship, nostalgia, running away, love—tended to be things everyone had experienced, feared, or fantasized about. The novel portrayed common elements of life in a way that could be commonly understood, something true even in the case of the more rebarbative texts of the avant-garde. *Malone Dies* or *The Waves* or *The Dead Father* may have taxed some peoples' patience, but they didn't really defeat anybody's powers of cognition; a few exceptions prove the rule that there's no such thing as "difficult fiction," an expression favored by people who never read anything truly difficult at all. Fundamentally, the novel implied that ordinary language and untutored insight furnished adequate devices for the understanding of individual life, and that prose was their proper medium. An economist or psychologist or sociologist would naturally possess a store of knowledge about his discipline, and therefore about the world, that a nonspecialist lacked, but the same scholar had to stand and face his own life—only one tidy corner of which could be illumined in technically economic, psychological, or sociological terms—with the same basic ignorance and amateurishness uniting everybody else, including the novelist. Even a middle-aged person too busy with work and family to read novels still knew that no other book than a novel could be written about his life that would do the least justice to that life in its complex way of taking place, as it had to, simultaneously in his head, in his household, in his society, and in history. The novel formed the shared culture of a literate secular society trying to apprehend life, or at least feeling that in principle life *could* be apprehended, through the medium of fictional narrative prose. Whatever far reaches of scholarship, analysis, introspection, or euphony any other variety of writing attained, there was as much justice as arrogance in what D.H. Lawrence said: "Being a novelist, I consider myself superior to the saint, the scientist, the philosopher, and the poet, who are all great masters of different bits of man alive, but never get the whole hog."

Lawrence's boast, however, made more sense in a culture where he could also refer to the novel as "the one bright book of life," where life itself could be pictured as essentially book-like and typographical rather than patterned after religious iconography (as in the past we've left behind) or flowing audiovisual imagery (as in the future we seem to have breached). A few days before this writing, Jonathan Franzen asked rhetorically, "Haven't we all secretly sort of come to an agreement, in the last year or two or three, that novels belonged to the age of newspapers and are going the way of newspapers, only faster?"

If the prevailing feeling is right and the novel—that *massif central* in the literary landscape of the last three hundred years—is sinking from view, its subsidence also indicates the submersion of an entire continent of mass literacy. The novel was the common ground of book readers. For it to become a marginal form (regardless of how many autobiographical novels, whose scenes and dialogues draw as much from invention as from memory, are classed as "memoirs") can only presage the marginalization of the amateur reading of book-length texts altogether, whether these appear as pixels on a screen or ink on paper. A literary culture without the novel at is center is likely to be a literary culture that isn't central to the broader culture either. Excellent long texts of all kinds will still be written, but these will form islands and archipelagoes off the digital mainland.

Can anything turn the tide? The solicitations of our attention made by streaming media and digital commentary seem too seductive for resistance to take hold on any mass scale. Many individuals and some communities and institutions will no doubt continue to choose a form of life in which awareness of the world is shaped more by the great invisible analytic categories of a bookish culture—history, society, psychology, and so forth: all things that can't be captured, except crudely, by any audiovisual recording technology or animated equivalent—but it would probably require a comprehensive revolution, in the socioeconomic sense, or widespread technological collapse, or else some combination of the two, for the decline of literature into parasitism and internal exile to be arrested. Even then, if the revolution were of the wrong kind, or the plunge into collapse too deep, mass literacy would only erode further.

In the meantime the culture of literature, as opposed to that of commentary, threatens to become a subculture instead, or, better, a counter-culture. This development alone would supply plenty of material and occasion for great writing, and even a quorum of readers. No one can deny the extraordinary achievements of vernacular writers in the fifteenth through seventeenth centuries, when mass literacy had barely begun to touch the countryside in which the vast majority of Europeans and North Americans still resided, and it's worth remembering that it took until roughly the middle of the nineteenth century before a majority of people could read even in protestant countries and in France. There is no reason to suppose that the waning of the graphosphere will be any less brilliant than the waxing. Still, the form and content, the scope and tone, the mode and manner of future great work will be marked by the valedictory situation in which literature now has to (silently, without moving its lips) pronounce its words.

MODES OF IMAGINING THE WRITER OF THE FUTURE

Lauren Groff

1.

The writer of the future will crouch in wind-swept aeries miles above the electronic din of the modern world, crafting feathers out of the leaves of old books.

Watch him strap the wings to his back and toddle to the nest's edge.

Watch the wind ruffle his fine, sparse hair as he tilts farther and farther into the abyss.

2.

At night, the writers of the future sleep but never dream. In the morning, their watchman arrives and flips on the lights, whistling under his breath. He carefully unrolls the writers' dust-cloths. The writers are bunched on a stainless steel table, their screens so thin that it is impossible to believe that they each contain the power of a million typing monkeys. The watchman flips their switches; the cursors blink on the screens; the writers hum to life; and by the time he emerges from the back room with his caffè mocha and ham sandwich, already one of the writers is printing out the first chapter in a multi-generational comedic masterpiece, destined to be hailed by a similar bank of critics of the future as "Powerful," "Luminous," "Finely Wrought," and "An Important Debut from a Writer to Watch."

3.

The writer of the future will sell her wares on the dog-crotted sidewalks of city streets, desperately flinging open her trench coat to reveal advance reading copies, braving the disgusted or averted faces of the more respectable kinds of pedestrians to whom French flaps or deckle edges mean nothing even remotely titillating.

4.

A writer of the future sits in her office in the present, trying very, very hard to not panic.

5.

Every year, the writers of the future will gather on a desert island, nervously clutching their notebooks to their chests and shuffling their spectacles on their noses. Over the course of two weeks, a series of competitions will take place in a great number of disciplines: Awkward Social Encounters, Furious Scribbling, Midnight Angst, Imperviousness to Blistering Reviews, Book Club Chatter, Esprit de L'Escalier, and Networking, among others. At the end of the Writer Olympics, points will be counted and the Bestsellers will be announced, and the losers will be shuffled one by one off the cliffs onto the jagged rocks below, notwithstanding some bitter muttering about how none of the judges even cracked the spines of the manuscripts under consideration.

6.

It will be mandated: At every table in every diner in the world, there will sit a writer about the size of a napkin dispenser. At the end of the meal, one shall put in one's credit card and out will pop a novel in a hundred and forty characters, or fewer.

Examples:

Bleak House: Fog in London, judicial shenanigans. How does it end? Nobody knows.

The Road: A boy and his father in black and white and red. And roasted babies!

Portnoy's Complaint: Oh, my penis. Oh, my mother. Oh, my penis again.

7.

A writer of the future holds her head in her hands.

8.

For a moment, the writer of the future stands backstage, listening to the roar of the crowd chanting her name, steeling herself for the inevitable barrage of panties and roses as soon as she emerges, hearing the nervous voices of her groupies whispering their *good lucks*, and knowing that while this part of the job isn't the easiest, all writers must deal with such crazed adulation at some point in their lives, and she can rest for the hour or so after her poetry reading in the carriage behind the six white stallions that will draw her slowly over the petal-strewn streets that will be, inevitably, thronged with her admirers shouting her own words back to her in soft and mellifluous tones.

9.

In America's brutal quest to compete with China to produce the best writers of the future, Baby Farms will sort infants into two distinct groups: Future Writers and Future Watchers of Television. The elite few will be ruthlessly prodded, tested, measured, and coached for the first thirty years of their lives, after which time they will have roughly five years to attempt to attain the status of Great American Novelist. If they fail, as of the eve of their thirty-sixth birthday, they will be forever afterward shuffled into these increasingly belittling categories: Promising Emerging Writer; Regional Writer; Midlist Writer; Catalog Copy Writer; Composition and Rhetoric Adjunct; Award-Winning Short Story Writer; Writer's Writer; Genre Writer; Self-Published Writer; and, last, and most ignominious, Hollywood Screenwriter.

10.

A writer of the future knows that no matter where she sets her work (in the historical-fiction past; in the science-fiction future), all she really is doing is talking about the present, anyway.

11.

The writer of the future comes into his study and shuts the door behind him. There are actual books on the shelves, to the frequent wonderment of his friends, who secretly decry the dust; the windows have darkened themselves at his entry; the coffee of the future has been instantly percolated and awaits his lips. He paces for a moment or two to listen to where he left off the day before. When the last words die down, he takes a deep breath and closes his eyes.

He unfolds his hands from the sleeves of the robes of the future. He lifts his elegant fingers. And he begins to conduct his words with vigorous armstrokes, the way a theremin player summons music from the air.

12.

If the writers of the future all look just like James Patterson, with their leathery jowls and sandy comb-overs, it is because they all are, as a matter of fact, genetically cloned replicas of James Patterson.

13.

All writers in the future, in order to be granted permission to publish their first books, will first have to collect a satisfactory number of previous careers. The Ministry of Arts and Letters, or Mini-Al, will issues little badges at the completion of stints in the occupations of: Food Server, Lifeguard, Transcriber for the Deaf, Rheumatologist, Data-Entry Clerk, Cashier, Sherpa, Furiously Disgusted Amazon Reviewer, Picketer, Pamphleteer, Census-Taker, Auditor, Policeperson, Interior Decorator, Groveling Toady to an Outsized Ego, and Over-consumer of Media Culture.

The writers who are at last allowed to become Writers sometimes sit in their mahogany-lined studies, behind locked doors, and dabble their fingers in the miniature waterfalls on their desks. They sigh, pace, and check that the door is locked. At last, they open their desk drawers, take out their little sashes with the badges stitched on them, and run loving fingers over each badge, in fond remembrance of those distant, awful times.

From a distance—say, through binoculars from an unmarked Mini-Al van in the street, or from the satellite that has turned its pulsing attention to that exact spot in the world—the writers who fondle their badges and wear fond, misty smiles on their faces often look like oversized Girl Scouts, beanies and all.

14.

The writer of the future will have her body surgically modified to fit the contours of her work, canting her spine forward so it hovers over her desk, bowing her hands to better fit the shape of a keyboard, and inserting a titanium shell under her epidermis so that she can take her agent's wise advice and grow a goddamn thicker skin already, jeez.

15.

A writer of the future shakes it off and continues on.

16.

Of all the many predictions that one can make about the writer of the future, there is only one that holds a whiff of the indisputable: that the writer of the future is the writer who writes. He is the one drawing word after word, pushing his sentences outward, into the darkness, into the thrilling unknown. He's not going to put it off for tomorrow, and he's not content with yesterday's work. He is the one alone somewhere, writing, right now. And right now. And right now.

THE BEST BOOKS WILL BE WRITTEN LONG AFTER YOU ARE DEAD

Rudolph Delson

Say it was 1910, and say on a breezy day you stopped me on Broadway, and say you asked me: "Sir, whither American letters?"

And say that the answer I gave you was fantastically correct. Say I predicted all about Modernism. Say I advised you to have your transatlantic agents ship you first editions of *Dubliners* (1914) and *The Voyage Out* (1915). Say I explained the plots and the modes of *The Great Gatsby* (1925) and *The Sun Also Rises* (1926) and *The Sound and the Fury* (1929), and say I did it incisively, with historical cross-references. Say I told you about, oh, Pearl Buck. And Saul Bellow and Toni Morrison. Say I even noted the late-century curios, the *Room Temperatures* (1990) and the *Autobiographies of Red* (1998). And say you were able to comprehend it all, not just the authors and the publication dates, but the meaning of all the millions: the mass migrations and the mass deaths and mass social movements, all the hours between Now and Then. How could you possibly have responded?

"Hum! *Portnoy's Complaint* sounds worth the while. You say it will be published in 1969? I do hope I survive to read it. I trust you when you say that there will be an influenza and that there will be horrid world-wide wars, and even so—even in peace and health—it is hard to imagine I shall live another fifty-nine years. And what a shame, too, because *Portnoy's Complaint* does sound ever so much better than *House of Mirth*. Or *The Golden Bowl*. To think, not only will there be a revolution, but it will be sexual."

"Sir," I would have said, "You can bide your time with *Moby-Dick*."

"I have never heard of any such thing."

"*Moby-Dick!* It was first published in 1851!"

"No, no, no. I have heard of no such thing."

We would have tipped hats, dodged the horse carriages, gone our ways—and although everything I told you would have been true, none of it would have improved your breezy day.

But it is not 1910.

It is 2010.

And here were are on Broadway, and the day is balmy. And here I am in my timesuit, a chrononaut from the unhappy year 2110, speaking to you through the electrical mouthpiece of my helmet, trying to keep my alien accent in check:

"Pay attention in 2014; that year will witness the publication of the first non-linear e-novel. It will appear on the internet, and it will advance the technique of Edward Packard in the rarest way imaginable. I said: Edward Packard. You have not read Edward Packard? But he invented *Choose Your Own Adventures*! What do you mean, you haven't read them? You have not ready any at all? But they were first published in 1979! Oh, it's a disgrace worse than Melville. In 2014, these non-linear e-novels, these online *Choose Your Own Adventures*, they will put an end to sequentially fixed narratives, and to sequentially bound print-publishing. It will be quite the biggest literary event since Aeschylus, or anyway since

Cervantes. Imagine if Proust had not had to fix his memories into any particular order: this is what will happen in 2014. Blossoms will bloom. And make certain to learn Spanish before 2021, because if you want to know anything about the American novel, you must read the works of Vilma Marielos Gonzalez Alvarado in the original. She will die young, of course—too young—when the tsunami from the first collapse of the Antarctic ice shelf scrubs out coastal California."

Or whatever.

You have gathered my point: There is no pleasure in knowing about novels; the pleasure is in reading them, and for that you must wait. And my other point: That as racy and as witty as it is to lay bets about the future of literary schools, and the future of publishing economics, and the future of authorial demographics, there is no glory in such guesswork, there is no glory in parlor games; the glory is all in the elucidation of human fate in elevated speech, the glory is all in literature itself. And my final point: That to the extent they were not written before we were born, most of the best books will be written only after you and I are both dead.

HOME WORD BOUND

Nancy Jo Sales

I once went to a party where the entertainment was a psychic; he took you off to a bedroom and relayed all the insights allegedly being whispered to him from on high. "You," he told me, "are surrounded by books." And he was right. Sometime in about the fourth grade, I became fairly obsessed with the amassing and reading of books, a sort of nervous condition which has never subsided. To this day I can't pass by a bookstore without breaking into jitters of anticipation, like an incorrigible horseplayer stumbling across an OTB. I have to go inside. My love of books has led me to do horrible things—I've stolen them from lovers and from libraries (though not for a long, long time). Today, bookshelves run around the upper walls of my apartment, housing thousands of titles. My desk is always piled high with them. So I literally am "surrounded by books," and have been for almost as long as I can remember.

And so this very real question of whether books will one day disappear altogether—due to technological advances or even environmental necessity—is of particular interest to me. Books are part of my identity, as much as my red hair or my big feet; I can't think of myself without them. As soon as I moved out of the house and was on my own, after college, I was lugging around boxes and boxes of paperbacks. (I've never been much interested in hardcovers—which are heavier—and don't consider myself a real collector of anything, except maybe words.) The older I get, the more boxes there are—on my last move, the grumbling moving men counted close to seventy cartons. My books have accumulated around me like a kind of history of my mind, of my experience and knowledge, however limited. Having them near me in a physical way serves as a reminder of who I am—like old photographs that you can actually re-enter, reliving the moment captured in the image.

I'll walk around my apartment now, randomly picking out volumes, and show you just what I mean. (I don't keep my books in any particular order, I have no system for arranging them—except possibly an aesthetic one: I put ones that look nice together next to each other—which I guess for me echoes something about the haphazardness of life, and the Quixotic ways of the brain.) Here is *Portnoy's Complaint* by Philip Roth. Ballantine Books edition, 1985. A pale yellow cover with a red and black title. I look at it, and I'm in New Haven and it's the spring of 1986. I have taken to my bed, an overstuffed futon. The linden trees outside my second-story window are in full bloom, fragrant. I have been crying. Someone has hurt me. A professor, who has dated his students often. It's my first experience with such villainy, and it hurts very badly. Ah, but this book is making me laugh. Here is Portnoy describing his father's battle with constipation: "I remember that when they announced over the radio the explosion of the first atom bomb, he said aloud, 'Maybe that would do the trick.'" I laugh and laugh. I cry some, still, but I become less sad and more taken with the playfulness and relentless verve of this writing. And, instructively, the character of Portnoy seems just the type of man to avoid in the future—never date a man who doesn't like his mother. I take a mental note to remember that.

Next, here is *The Pillow Book of Sei Shonagon*. A Penguin Classic, 1984. The cover is a detail from the Genji Scroll of a kimono-wearing flutist in the Heian court. Sei Shonagon was a tenth-century lady-in-waiting in the court of the Japanese Empress Teishi, as well as a freethinking sort of diva and a great writer. I am reading her many trenchant observations ("Things without merit: an ugly person with a bad character"), riding a packed commuter train through Tokyo; it's 1988. I've come to Japan to teach Japanese salarymen English conversation. I've come to find something I've never encountered before, and Tokyo, with its streets full of bobbing colorful umbrellas and neon pachinko parlors and steaming yakitori carts, is providing me with that. Every image, every moment here is like a poem or a line from a poem—Japan is like a poem in the way it breaches understanding, in how alternately kitschy and elegantly beautiful it is. "Elegant things," Shonagon writes. "Plum blossoms covered with snow . . ." I will do a lot of bad writing here, and I'll read a lot of books about Japan, which I'll take with me when I go back to America. "Pleasing things," writes Shonagon. "Finding a large number of tales that one has not read before."

Here is one more example: Herbert Asbury's *The Gangs of New York: An Informal History of the New York Underworld*, a book I dragged around with me for years before ever reading it. This happens with books sometimes; it's almost as if they are waiting for you to be ready to receive them. And if you didn't have them on hand, would you ever discover them? It's a question that goes back to the classic debate between the Katharine Hepburn and Spencer Tracy characters in *The Desk Set* (1957). She's a research librarian with a belief in the mystical relationship between books and a woman's mind; he's a computer salesman with a single-minded confidence in the power of machines to replace human thought. The upshot, of course, is that they fall in love: an inevitable compromise to an impossible-to-resolve conundrum.

I had just moved into an apartment on Water Street in Manhattan, in the fall of 1999, when I finally decided to pull *The Gangs of New York* (Dorset Press edition, 1989) down off the shelf because, suddenly, I was living in the neighborhood it was about—not just the neighborhood, but one of the actual buildings on one of the very streets, the first stretch of Water Street after the Brooklyn Bridge. I learned—while eating apples on my daybed—that in the 1850s (pre-bridge), this same street was said to be the most dangerous street, not just in the country, but in the world. One of the buildings, known as the Old Brewery, saw a murder a night! "Fights were of almost constant occurrence," Asbury wrote, "and there was scarcely an hour of the day or night when drunken orgies were not in progress; through the flimsy, clapboard walls could be heard the crashing thud of brickbat or iron bar, the shrieks of the unhappy victims, the wailing of starving children . . ." And so from this horrific chaos rose the first gangs of New York—the Plug Uglies and Shirt Tails and Dead Rabbits.

Walking my big dog, Boo, through the neighborhood at dusk, it was as if I could hear these ghostly gang members pounding down the cobblestones in pursuit of each other. I had spent the last few years following the exploits of some private school gangs for *New York* magazine. They were a very different lot—poseurs, wannabes, you could say—but they had bonded together for many of the same reasons as the real life Bowery Boys: because they felt lost, because they needed a family. I knew then that if—when—I ever wrote a book, it would be about these kids. One day, when my eyes go scanning across the bookshelves in my apartment, I'll see my own book among the titles. Anyway, that's where I always imagine it.

Would my life in books have been the same if they had been coming to me via Kindle or iPad? I don't think so. There's something about the physicality of a book, the way it looks and feels and even smells—the notes written in the margins—that makes it a living, breathing companion (who, like yourself, is actually dying). I don't think books will ever disappear for this reason: We need them too much. They remind us that we exist; they show us how we have lived. At least, that's what they have done for me ever since I was a nine-year-old girl growing up in Miami. Every Saturday, my mother would give me the five dollars I had earned by doing various chores, and I would immediately jump on my purple banana-seat bike and ride to the Walden Books on Miracle Mile. And it was a long way from my house.

SURVIVAL TIPS FOR WRITERS (AND BOOKS IN GENERAL): A LIST

Katherine Taylor

1.

Try to be from someplace awful like Fresno. This will give you the drive and ambition you'll need to work hard and escape. If possible, your parents should be sophisticated enough to appreciate that they have raised an artist and just rich enough to bail you out when you can't pay your rent or when your car needs new tires because you got drunk at lunch and drove over the median on Highland.

2.

Don't go back to Fresno.

3.

Write stories you think might make the people you know angry. Use personal details (the more top-secret the better). In the tertiary subplot to your first novel, include the conversation you had with your best friend Gretchen after she discovered her husband's homosexual infidelity. Include the part where Gretchen said, "But I really don't think that means he's gay." Later, after your book comes out, when Gretchen tells you in a four-page email that she no longer wants to be friends with you, conclude without a doubt that she is just jealous of your success.

4.

Have no trouble whatsoever writing your second novel. Write for an audience. Here is a (partial) list of people you might write for: people you need to forgive, girls in dresses in train stations, divorced teachers on beaches, Gretchen, the newscaster eating alone at the bar, the actor backstage with an hour before his next scene, thirty-eight-year-old women with broken hearts, twenty-four-year-old women with broken hearts, fourteen-year-old girls with broken hearts, babysitters. The woman in her Range Rover crying at the stop light on Sunset, people on airplanes, people on subways, people in three-day blackouts in northern Michigan, alcoholics in ski lodges who have broken ankles, American back-packers in Europe, European tourists in Hollywood, poets, land-lords, nannies, gardeners, five-year-olds, shrinks, housewives, men alone in sushi bars, women alone in French restaurants at lunch, unemployed college graduates in Central Park at midday, entry-level Citigroup employees in Central Park at midday, lonely bloggers, graduate students in the arts and sciences, painters, men who are divorced and live in big empty houses, my mom. Drinkers who want to feel less drunk than Kingsley Amis. Fresno Armenians, Fresno WASPs, quarterbacks from Fresno State who go on to become coaches at USC, big fat men in love with silent beautiful women, men called Roland, teenagers with insomnia, victims of unrequited love, star-crossed lovers, step-daughters, step-mothers, baby brothers, middle children, only children, children of astronauts, sons whose fathers didn't come to see them play in the varsity tennis state championships, the high school calculus teacher who knows that his students are cheating but who's kind of impressed by their ingenuity, zookeepers, cyclists, and bartenders.

5.

Fall in love with someone who lives at least 3,000 miles away. Don't let something as unpredictable as people interfere with your work. When you do fall in love, try to find a banker or a mathematician—someone who thinks the life of a writer is exotic and exciting. Encourage this illusion for as long as possible. When the mathematician says to you one morning at six as you walk from his house in Brooklyn Heights to the subway together so that he can make his early meeting in midtown, "How does it feel to get up in the morning like someone who works for a living?" realize that the illusion may have turned against you. Accept that the relationship may be doomed, and start scavenging for details you can use in your work.

6.

Read a lot of Calvin Trillin. Read *About Alice*. You will always need to read a bit of Calvin Trillin, and you will always need to read *About Alice*. If Calvin Trilin makes you feel bad intellectually, go to the movies so that you can feel superior.

7.

If your neck hurts, it's because your tennis racquet is too heavy. Pain in the back or the neck has nothing to do with sitting at your desk for fourteen hours a day. Maybe if you played less tennis and did more writing, your neck wouldn't hurt so much. Maybe you should work harder.

8.

Don't turn on the television, or you may never turn it off. If you must watch college football, plan to watch it with friends, preferably in a bar called Big Wang's on the corner of Selma and Cahuenga that serves tater tots smothered in Alfredo sauce and bacon. Get there early in the morning so you can make the most of their all-you-can-drink-build-it-yourself-Bloody-Mary-bar. Leave after the third game, or after the toilet in the women's bathroom starts to overflow. Go back to your friend Anne's house, because she lives nearby and has a big television she never watches. Make as many friends as possible who have the self-control to not watch reruns of the 2005 US Open quarterfinal between Andre Agassi and James Blake (as you would do if you had a TV of your own), but who don't mind if you stop by on a Saturday afternoon to engage them in the Stanford–USC matchup. Choose friends most likely to appreciate the fraught narrative of USC's freshman quarterback. Be smart.

9.

Walk everywhere. It's cheaper and it reduces your chances of getting a DUI.

10.

Pretend you never have to worry about money. Ignore the utilities and the phone bill until they actually turn off your phone. Then call up the phone company and be really nice. They'll let you pay your bill in teeny-tiny bits! They appreciate you as a customer! Eat inexpensive boxes of quinoa and pasta because they're delicious. Wear the same clothes you wore in college. Let people think you are an eccentric artist who doesn't have time to think about clothes. Whatever you do: Never think about the clothes your roommates stole from you at Groton (that will just make you sick). Never buy new shoes, but have the old ones repaired at the very cheap guy on East 73rd Street between Second and First Avenue.

11.

You're not home until you unpack your books. You may think to yourself when you get to Brussels, "I'm home!" but you may not get round to unpacking your books. You might move from Rome to Los Angeles after you've called off your engagement one month before the wedding, and you might think to yourself, "Los Angeles is home!" But if there's no room for your books, and you put them in storage, you are susceptible to falling in love with someone in New York, and when that's not right either, you must realize that books are your commitment. Find someplace to put your books. Stay there. Sit down. Write. Repeat.

THE EXTENT OF OUR DECLINE

Kyle Beachy

"He pictured precise objects, he made them briefly shine
with immanence, a bowl for food, a spoon constructed out
of thought, perception, memory, feeling, and imagination."
—Don DeLillo, *Mao II*

1.

Let's recall the letter Horace addressed to Augustus 2,000 years
back, in which the poet laments the decline of literature. And let's
imagine Augustus sitting in his private library, the world's most
important man surrounded by towering columns and much
papyrus, the midday sun burning golden through tall arches, its
light busy with dust. The emperor looks exactly like the busts we
see of him. After an hour spent leaning over Book II of Horace's
Ars Poetica, Augustus rises, stretches, and moves into the hall, a
man gravid with thought. But then, reaching the garden, he begins
to chuckle. Something, it seems, has struck him as funny, and soon
the Emperor is so consumed by mirth he's forced to sit on a nearby
bench. He's bellowing as only an emperor can! He smacks an impe-
rious knee and speaks upward, as if to the wind, "Oh, my poor
friend! Just wait for the iPad!" Guffaw, guffaw as guards nearby
crack their own sly smiles. "You and your kind are fucked, Horace!"

2.

Horace, who had the benefit of steady patronage from the good Gaius Maecenas, would be fine. He had a cozy estate in the hills of modern Tivoli in which to sit and ponder life's more elusive virtues. It would be the distant heirs to his tradition who would face rather more difficult circumstances.

Today's poets strike me as heroic, standing as they do among the enlightened creators who know well to expect nary a dime for their art. Perhaps a dime. There's little space for illusion inside the pursuit of poetry, and the work, for better or worse, is created by and large free of the burden of the potential jackpot.

We novelists, though, have long suffered from a common delusion that if all goes perfectly right, if stars and popular taste and film options align just so, we'll find ourselves living fat, perhaps tearing through Horace's backyard in something small and fast and European, while Natalie Portman rides shotgun, her hands full with aged cheese and salami, a bottle of Brunello waiting in her lap. Fantasies, admittedly, have varied. But the novel, with its formal capacity to tap into our American cultural mainline, has maintained at least the promise of sweeping import.

Except now our noble industry has shrunk before our eyes; the parties are smaller and the rooftops lower. Certain loud voices break the news that the novel is stupid, anyway, and prominent journalists and memoirists applaud loudly. Our elders, shuddering a bit at the prospect of change, nod and grumble. It's been dead before, but never like this. Then it turns out that Portman is vegan, and a Foer fan as well; Apple is cornering an already-cornered market, and the sky tears and bleeds upon our poor, novelist shoulders. We stand and drip, confused.

3.

Horace's concern was the decline of his art. Poets, he feared, were wandering off track or growing lazy, thus failing the Roman Empire they were paid to serve.

Today's alarm is rather this fear's inversion—a matter of the world changing beyond the reach of our preferred mode of expression. The zeitgeist shifts from psychology to neurology, mind to body, accelerating always and rendering the long form of written narrative—with its naive characters and plot conventions and mimetic impulses—both too demanding and too *composed* to befit the madhouse reality of our time.

There is a kind of giddy excitement about it all; enthusiasms are fleeting but constantly replaced. Today novelty has all the endurance of a single breath; an idea once shared transforms (or metastasizes, if we respect the viral metaphor) into an idea known to everyone, making newness the primary focus of our shared cultural narrative: feed me stories of old technologies dying, reaffirm my standing on the frontier of what's new, then newer, then newer still, and I'll happily burn whatever stale relics I find inside my house.

Which of us doesn't want to be told that the age we live in is unique?

We know by now that as few as five hours on the internet alters the brain itself, training it to absorb data ever more rapidly, quick lessons gleaned from many sources. Our patterns of data ingestion have shifted away from sustained devotion to a single source. I like to show my students screen-caps of CNN broadcasts from the early '90s—the anchor sitting behind her desk, a single graphic floating over her shoulder. No partitions or scrolling bars. No data cramped into corners. The students yawn. Compared to the packed screenspace we see now, there's an almost pastoral simplicity to the old screen, a spatial naiveté or hubristic wastefulness.

And now. Just look at these poor pages. Yellow and old, they smell of a death that is almost assuredly their own.

4.

If only Horace were here to clarify for us the complicated relationship between a novel and its pages. Clearly, the novel is built around the mechanics of the book. But to conflate the two is a mistake both easy and terrible. Phillip Roth makes this mistake by grumpily declaring it cultic, the sort of thing that in twenty-five years will be read by only "a small group of people. Maybe more people than now read Latin poetry, but somewhere in that range." For Roth, the novel is the book is the novel, a singular and static object whose death he hears rattling over even his aging characters' own.

The grandiose *Alinea* cookbook and Kathryn Regina's tiny, perfect *I Am in the Air Right Now* prove the obvious point that books are plural. The acts of their reading are vastly different, and neither are *novels*, this floating term we're so intent to preface with the definite article, a homogenous form. But just as the LP has been packaged in multiple media—vinyl, eight-track, cassette, CD, and shapeless, intangible data files, while vinyl perseveres—so too is the novel capable of movement between media. Novelists have much to learn from the vinyl record's stamina, like the practice of including a free download with every purchase. One LP in two distinct forms: the tangible (beautiful, sensuous, justly fetishized) vinyl, and intangible (sterile, erasable, but infinitely portable) data file.

But even such objective plurality wouldn't quiet the loudest of the death alarmists, like *Esquire*'s Tom Junod. Best known for his research into the identity of the "Falling Man" in Richard Drew's famous photograph, Junod casts his ongoing obituary in language that would make Roth proud, calling the novel, "that ever-more elaborate cathedral with the ever-more precipitously declining attendance." Junod's larger argument is contained inside his scathing review of DeLillo's *Falling Man*: "the idea that when the planes hit and the buildings went down we entered the 'age of nonfiction,' when journalism . . . is able to grasp what's happened to us more than fiction can, even fiction by our most accomplished and ambitious writers."

There's an irony to Junod's attack, considering that its target is an author who has always recognized his novels' inability to encompass his subject, which is nothing short of American life in the twentieth century. Each of DeLillo's novels reaches for media beyond its own text for effect: the famous television of *White Noise*; the films that bookend both *Players* and *Point Omega* and serve as plot engines for *Americana, Running Dog*, and *The Names*; the performance art of *The Body Artist* and *Falling Man*; spectacle and photography in *Mao II* and *Underworld*; journalism and official government record in *Libra*; the mathematics and cosmology of *Ratner's Star*; and even sport and music in *End Zone* and *Great Jones Street*. For DeLillo, the project of the novel has always been to destroy the idea of author as sole proprietor of meaning. Today, of course, access to such multi-media is the basic domain of even our simplest handheld devices, and this might explain why his fiction doesn't cut with the same acuity it did twenty short (but seemingly infinite) years ago.

The purview of the novel continues to be pinched from outside, and perhaps rightly so. Today, the services the novel once claimed as its sole territory are more readily provided by other sources. Satire has been exploded by *The Daily Show, The Onion*, and a thousand blogs updated hourly. The same goes for expressions of tragedy, loss, and sometimes redemption, these subjects all locked up within the memoir's wheelhouse. Even knowledge itself, information of almost any sort: Who today reads a novel to learn when Wikipedia offers the shorter, more condensed version?

Regarding our "age of nonfiction," Junod finds an equally ardent partner in David Shields. In one of the roughly 6,000 promotional interviews he gave to support the release of *Reality Hunger*, Shields fired endless rounds at the fictional: "Living as we perforce do in a manufactured and artificial world, we yearn for the 'real' [to] break through the clutter ... More invention, more fabrication, aren't going to do this."

But Shields is certainly no Horace, and is much more Nero or Caligula than Augustus. One big reason Shields doubts that he's "the only person finding it more and more difficult to read or write novels" is precisely the same reason that the novels he did write aren't terribly compelling. It's a reason Shields doesn't seem particularly interested in hiding, which is, worded one way, that David Shields is an asshole. Or, more accurately: David Shields doesn't believe in communion.

5.

Here the past, yet again, proves valuable. In 1898 Tolstoy defined art as "that human activity which consists in one man's consciously conveying to others by certain external signs the feelings he has experienced, and in others being infected by those feelings and also experiencing them." This is communion, which is also catharsis—art as exercise for the empathetic muscles that define us as human. If the novel has ceded ground to other entertainments, it maintains a distinct and formal advantage in the realm of communion.

Our analogue lives demand and require analogue art, an expression that goes beyond the ones and zeros of our machines. What better form than the novel to capture the gradients of madness that define a modern life? For madness, and our understanding of it, depends on its presentation, the language attached to it, the progresses by which we see it emerge and abate. The novelist's task is to share perspectives in ways other writers simply cannot. To move between them and ply their differences, establish similarities we'd otherwise miss. To both trigger and conduct a reader's own empathy.

Memoirists, political pundits, music critics, rock stars, athletes, manifesto writers, internationally acclaimed clothing designers . . . from these figures we allow for, even expect, egomania, self-promotion, and hyper-criticality of all who differ from them. But novelists increasingly exhibit these same traits, and never has it been easier to set a novel down; sit an asshole behind the fun-house's control levers and I will happily walk away.

Today's novel has to be an exercise of both the mind and heart, physical at times like a finger in the eye. I'm not sure I can any longer cringe in response to film, but I do regularly when reading long fiction. This cringe is *effect*, feeling, something increasingly rare and thus a reward. It is a process whose effect is unnamed and untraceable via MRI but is a novelist's true and vital gift, the reason Sven Birkets, in his comprehensive essay "Reading in a Digital Age," so passionately insists, "My reading has done a great deal for me even if I cannot account for most of it."

This gift, defined solely by the process through which it is achieved, is possible only over time. This is the novel's value, and what must be its future.

Consider the account of head trainer/panhandler Barry Loach, which David Foster Wallace, our paragon of novelistic communion, saved until page 967 of *Infinite Jest*. Wallace devotes only four pages to Loach's story, or roughly 0.3 percent of the giant novel, and yet he contains inside this brief narrative of physical communion his novel's giant thumping heart, a small, profound reward for the long, arduous task of reading his novel, proof of the author's respect, even love, for his reader.

Here is your novel of the future. It is messy and sometimes long.

It traffics in both ontology and epistemology and demands from you, reader, a level of engagement unique today. Your time, your patience. Your effort. But rest assured, please, that beneath these words are the everlasting arms. Sink into these pages, the novelist says, whether on paper or touchscreen, and find love within. Lies, yes, told via a bounty, even superfluity, of words. Though hidden among these lies is an experience buried, a truth untellable as fact.

You'll likely forget where you heard it, but that's not really the point.

ENDURING LITERATURE

Joshua Gaylord

I read James Joyce's *Ulysses* for the first time as a freshman in college at UCLA. I remember the experience of the book—not just the content, but the physical book itself. It was the Hans Walter Gabler edition, published just four years before, and the cover featured simply the title of the book and the author's name highlighted by blocks of primary color—as though the typography itself were the key: as though the printed words were the treasure. It was a big book, solid and cumbersome, the gravity of the text itself paralleled by the way it felt in my backpack—a leaden weight made heavier by the two other books I carried along with it to assist my reading: Don Gifford's annotations on *Ulysses* (as big as *Ulysses* itself) and Stuart Gilbert's blissfully mass-market-sized discourse on *Ulysses*.

That's right: I was reading three books in order to read one book.

I carried those books around for months. My back hurt, my shoulders ached. I had to requisition one of the larger tables in the campus cafeteria to spread out all three books so I could refer back and forth among them—all while eating lunch with my non-page-turning hand. I wasn't just a reader of Joyce, I was an arsenal of Joyce, and you could spot me in all my erudite pretension, cheeseburger in hand, a mile away. I moved slowly, and literature was something not just of the mind but also of the muscles.

The "future of books" naturally calls to mind images of the Kindle or some other e-book reader: volumes of literature toted around in the form of thin plastic tablets. The evolution and popularity of such technology seem contingent upon one notion: that literature should be easier to experience. The questions at stake seem to revolve around the assumption that the goal is to interface with literature as smoothly as possible. Is the e-book reader light enough to be carried in a purse, backpack, or briefcase without adding to anyone's daily burden? Is the screen crystal clear? Is the contrast sharp enough to be easy on the eyes? Are e-books immediately available, so that the user will never have to travel to a bookstore? Are the page-turning buttons ergonomically positioned to prevent the user from having to exert too much energy navigating through the text?

I wonder what my own experience of reading *Ulysses* would have been if I had read it on a Kindle—maybe even with hyperlinks to Gifford's annotations and Gilbert's critical perspectives. At the risk of sounding too much like an Andy Rooney–type curmudgeon, it's hard for me to picture James Joyce's *Ulysses* being contained adequately in a thin slab of sophisticated plastic.

Maybe it has something to do with the gradual shift away from book fetishization. Maybe all those voices that decried the transfer of music from pressed vinyl (with a texture you could feel with your fingertips!) to manageable but abstract data files are the same voices that will now lament the passing of books with actual pages you can smell, and ink that comes off on your hands.

But, for me, it's not so much about the satisfaction of holding something tangible in my hands. Instead, it's about the way I've always perceived reading—and reading great literature in particular.

Here's the thing: I don't think I want reading to be *easy*.

The books that have had the greatest impact on my life are not the ones that entertained me the most—rather, they're the ones I've had to *endure*. *Ulysses* wasn't a "good read"—it was a project, a mission, a brief military stint undertaken by a strong-willed, idealistic youth. It was a labor to carry, it required innumerable accoutrements to be read (not just the two other texts but also a notebook and a pen, a highlighter, slips of scrap paper to mark particular pages). Even the page design was more an opponent than a partner: There were line numbers on each page. Line numbers! This book wasn't kidding around. Reading it, you felt you were staring down the business end of Literature.

But to arrive at the end of a book like that—to complete the project of reading it—there is for me no greater satisfaction. Wracked, enlightened, tortured, exhausted, bettered, you come out the other side of a book like *Ulysses* feeling as though you've had an experience, as though you have actually, actively *read*. And there are, for those of us who enjoy such literature of endurance, many authors who write books like bricks you could use to build a sound shelter for the three little pigs: William Gaddis, John Barth, Doris Lessing, Thomas Pynchon, Neal Stephenson, David Foster Wallace (to mention just a few of the most recent examples). Granted, there are some big books that make you feel, as you close them, that they haven't quite been worth the effort. For me, that's the risk that makes the expedition all the more thrilling.

It's possible that books are like relationships. Some people may be quite happy hopping from one book to the next, looking for easy reads in the same way you might troll the bars for easy lays. There are thousands of completely forgettable books that will amuse you for an evening or two; they seduce you with their market-tested cover art, their comfortable length (not to overwhelm commitment-phobes), even the unabashedly lewd pick-up lines that open their narratives, the lines referred to in writing workshops as "hooks": *The summer my dog died, I learned how to stop time.*

Don't get me wrong, you can have a great time whoring around with books like this for quite a while. But I like a bit of a challenge in my reading life—more of a commitment. Eventually, after a few of your one-night stands, your eye might be caught by an opening sentence like this one:

> From a little after two oclock until almost sundown of the long still hot weary dead September afternoon they sat in what Miss Coldfield still called the office because her father had called it that—a dim hot airless room with the blinds all closed and fastened for forty-three summers because when she was a girl someone had believed that light and moving air carried heat and that dark was always cooler, and which (as the sun shone fuller and fuller on that side of the house) became latticed with yellow slashes full of dust motes which Quentin thought of as being flecks of the dead old dried paint itself blown inward from the scaling blinds as wind might have blown them.
>
> —William Faulkner, *Absalom, Absalom!*

In the future of reading, I wonder if such an opening line will characterize a book as the awkward, nerdy, neurotic girl drinking Diet Dr. Pepper and tugging on her split ends. This book could potentially offer a vast, complex, wholly satisfying experience— but you know from the start that such a relationship is going to be a long-term one, and that it's going to require work.

I once had a relationship with William H. Gass's *The Tunnel*. It was a difficult couple of months. We didn't get along—even though on the surface it seemed we would be a perfect couple. It was certainly no *Ulysses*. But I stuck with it to the very end, searching for any glimmer of connection or love, so sure was I that there must be one. At the very last, however, we parted quietly, with little fanfare, a bit embarrassed at our failure to make it work.

Do I wish that book were easier to read?

No. I admire its depths, even though I was not the one meant to plumb them.

Do I wish that book were shorter?

No. I respect a book that respects itself—a book that is not ashamed of declaring itself in bold and profuse terms.

Do I regret having spent time reading it?

Not at all. What I wanted was not entertainment but an experience—and I got that experience, and it has stayed with me. I feel that *The Tunnel* and I accomplished something, and I am reminded of that accomplishment whenever I see the book resting, still admired and enduring, on my bookshelf.

As for the future of literature: In my more pessimistic moments, I see it as a gradual softening over time. Not as a dumbing down—I don't see the world becoming less intelligent or intellectual, but rather simply less patient. In my most dystopian nightmares, I picture literature packaged so conveniently that you could consume it like a vitamin pill—without even having to take the trouble to read it.

On the other hand, it bears mentioning that the era of difficult reading is not entirely past—and that certain contemporary authors have taken up the mantle. Dave Eggers, for example, seems to have launched an entire industry of literature wrapped in challenging packaging. I remember picking up a paperback edition of his *Heartbreaking Work of Staggering Genius* and discovering that he had put fine print addenda in every possible location, including the copyright page. He had included a long and somewhat rambling introduction that I felt obligated to read before I got to the (much more readable) primary text. And there was another whole section at the back that required the reader to turn the book literally upside-down in order to sift through the tiny print and even tinier footnotes of the appendix.

Even in the world of graphic novels, which, we assume, should be *easier* to read than traditional novels, we are offered authors like Chris Ware, whose pictorial stories are challenging to navigate on the page and are interlaced with, again, fine print narrative that resists perusal by any but the most dedicated (or self-punishing) of readers.

If you are a completist when it comes to books—the kind of reader who must exhaust every corner and niche before you consider a book fully read—then these texts offer a particular challenge. They seem to be made for the bibliophile. I am heartened by such books.

Maybe liking books is different from liking reading, the two things only arbitrarily related by their physical proximity—a proximity becoming increasingly less common. And maybe it's possible to be an aficionado of one without the other. Maybe books and reading should, ultimately and always, be considered separately.

And maybe if, in the future, it will become ever more common to enjoy reading without books, maybe it will become equally common to enjoy books without reading.

I have a copy of Gilbert Sorrentino's *Mulligan's Stew* on my bookshelf, purchased many years ago from a used bookstore. It is big and dusty, and the pages are yellowed. I've never read it, and something tells me I never will. But it's there, and I like having it there, and many times I've taken it down and flipped through the pages and felt the thing to be eminently *worthy* as an object, even if unread. It has survived two relocations to different households, and I'm sure I'll carry it with me for the rest of my life.

I know exactly where it lives on my bookshelves. Even if I were blind, I could lead you right to it.

There it is. It exists. There's no question.

Like a living thing, it has a spine.

AN INTERVIEW WITH TOM PIAZZA
ON THE FUTURE OF THE BOOK

Tom Piazza

The Questioner arrives at room 204 of the London Lodge, on the outskirts of New Orleans, the hotel room where he is scheduled to meet with Tom Piazza, author of the novels *City of Refuge* and *My Cold War*, the nonfiction collection *Devil Sent the Rain*, and a writer for the HBO series *Treme*, to discuss the future of the book. Knocking once, twice, he receives no answer. The Questioner tries the door and finds it unlocked. Walking into the room he finds Piazza asleep in his street clothes on an unmade bed, with books stacked on the floor, on the couch, on the coffee table, and a small child's record player emitting a ticking sound as the needle goes around the inner spiral of a long-finished LP side. The Questioner replaces the record player's tone arm on its perch and shuts the machine off. Pulling the desk chair up to the side of the bed, the Questioner tentatively reaches out to shake the sleeping figure by the shoulder.

Tom Piazza: (*still asleep; shifting slightly in bed*) Three bucks's too much . . .

Questioner: Mr. Piazza . . .

TP: (*shifts more, frowns, groans*)

Q: We're here to talk about the future of the book.

TP: (*waking up*) . . . huh?

Q: The future of the book . . . your thoughts . . . ?

TP: What the fuck are you talking about?

Q: Uh . . . we discussed this . . . ? You were going to . . .

TP: What do you mean by "book"? Where are my glasses . . .

Q: We can come back some other time, if this . . .

TP: Here they are. How did my glasses get on the floor? (*picks up an envelope from the nightstand, shakes it slightly, plucks out two small pieces of what appears to be rock candy, and places them under his tongue*) Okay—which book are you talking about, now?

Q: You were going to give us a few words about the future of the book. For a . . . book.

TP: Right, right. (*sits up; opens nightstand drawer; pulls out a .38 pistol*) I assume I can define the word "book" any way I want to, since you won't define it for me?

Q: (*alarmed, staring at gun*) Yes, certainly . . .

TP: Okay. (*significantly more alert*) I'll skip all the usual drainage about electronic books and the death of publishing and how many cookbooks get published and how hard it is to sell midlist fiction. And how important literature is, and how we tell ourselves stories to make sense of our lives, or how in the future we'll all be able to write our own endings to books, as if we can't do that already, or whether backlit screens will replace regular LCDs on the new Zorro e-reader . . . You don't need me for that crap. I really don't care anyway. I'm old school.

Q: (*still staring at the .38*) Meaning . . . ?

TP: Meaning first of all that I like books that I can hold in my hand. Made of paper. I don't need to plug them in, and I don't have to buy batteries for them. They look different from each other, and I like that. I like looking at *Bleak House* and being able to tell that it embodies a different sense of life than *Jesus' Son* does. I like carrying the fuckers around with me. One weighs more than the other. If you like to read your books on an Etch A Sketch, that's fine with me. Especially if you're reading my books. But it's like looking at a book of paintings where *Guernica* is the same size as a Holbein portrait. You get no sense of the scale of things, of the nature of the artist's ambition.

Q: Isn't ambition a little . . . corny?

TP: (*raises .38; cocks hammer*) I'm sorry; would you care to repeat that?

Q: I said, "Ambition makes me horny."

TP: (*lowering .38*) Yeah, me too. I want to talk about novels right now, because that's what I write.

Q: You're also writing for TV, aren't you?

TP: (*angrily; defensively*) Yeah—so what? Besides, it's not TV; it's HBO . . .

Q: (*holding up hands*) Nothing wrong with that. Just checking.

TP: Computers and e-books and smartphones all basically look alike. They are strictly vehicles; you pick them up to step through them into some consensus reality; you're wired in. Everything is leveled out. When everything has equal weight, everything is weightless. The world they offer is one of infinitely diverse information with a common denominator: the screen. The computer is neutral in that it gives you access to limitless amounts of information, but the one requirement is that you have to get it on the computer. The information has no smell, no weight, no texture. Nothing that seriously impinges on your reality. People think it represents some kind of democratizing of information because everything's the same size. But democracy is when things of different sizes get a chance to mix it up and work it out, measure themselves in their respective strengths. If everything is the same size, there's no perspective. Perspective, as in, you know, painting. Everything becomes two-dimensional, flat . . .

Q: Isn't perspective an illusion? A person's face looming close to the viewer might appear larger than a skyscraper in the distance . . .

TP: Exactly. But that tells you something about reality. Whereas if you had a little chart where you could see everything rendered in exact relative scale but boiled down to a fifteen-inch frame, it might tell you something factual, but you wouldn't have an experience. You wouldn't learn something about the reality that something small near at hand can have a much larger impact than something large far away . . .

Q: Well . . . whatever. So what about the novel?

TP: I'm coming to that. A novel makes a world from one writer's perspective. It offers point of view, in the specialized literary sense, which is to say that it places point of view in a contrasting context. The writer makes the point of view, maybe multiple points of view, and also makes the context for those points of view. You make a world. A computer is a competing kind of world; it's an anti-world. The computer's ambition is to transcend point of view entirely.

Q: (*gaining confidence*) But what about all the chat rooms and discussion boards and social networking sites? There are a lot of points of view offered there.

TP: There are a lot of points of view being offered right now down in a dozen bars outside on Airline Highway, but very little perspective. Their dynamic is about letting off steam. If you want to cook something you have to keep the oven closed for a while, otherwise it will be half-baked. Nobody really works anything out at the corner bar. They just confirm their own assumptions. They think they have a point of view because they're arguing with somebody. But perspective means arguing with yourself. Two eyes, set in different locations on your face, make 3-D. Thelonious Monk used to say, "Two is one." That's what he meant.

Q: I'm having trouble following you.

TP: Yeah . . . right . . . well, I guess it boils down to some people like books and some people don't.

Q: But you're making a case for one over the other.

TP: I'm not, really. I'm just saying they're different.

Q: I mean, why is that important? Why is it important whether you get your information from a computer of some sort or from a physical book?

TP: (*regarding the questioner appraisingly*) The information is qualitatively different, isn't it? Isn't there some sort of meta-information in the weight of a book, in the effort and time it takes to produce it, as opposed to just hitting a button and sending your latest notion off into the internet? There's a resonance. Somebody else might have held the book, and valued it. Maybe they made notes in the margin, and kept it and handed it down to their children . . . I mean, you can give somebody a book; it has weight, it's a gesture of faith in the future. The message of the internet is that the moment is what matters; the closer you can get to that virtual moment, the closer you are to reality. But a novel offers perspective; it says time curves and things change, and what looks big now might really be small, and vice-versa, and here's a model of how that works . . . I mean, if there's no future for books, there's no future . . . People who are interested in time and have a taste for the individual consciousness up against mass consensus will always have a taste for books.

Q: So that's your prediction about the future of books?

TP: (*annoyed*) Look, I don't know about the fucking future. Nobody knows what's going to happen in ten seconds.

Q: (*exasperated*) Oh, that is ridiculous; everybody is obsessed with it. There are tens of thousands of websites dedicated to making guesses about the future ... (*gasping*) Dear God ... what are you doing?

TP: (*points the .38 at the questioner and tightens his index finger on the trigger*) I've just about had it with this conversation.

Q: Please ... don't shoot.

TP: (*pulls trigger; flame sprouts from the tip of the gun. It is a gag-store cigarette lighter*)

Q: (*shaking, wiping forehead with a kerchief*) Jesus ... what is wrong with you?

TP: Oh, come on. You saw that coming, didn't you?

WHY IT MAY TAKE ME A WHILE TO RETURN YOUR EMAIL

Garth Risk Hallberg

"To alcohol: the cause of, and solution to, all of life's
problems."   —Homer Simpson

From: neuroticnovelist@redacted.com
To: enhanceyourpenis@hotmail.com
Date: Mon June 10, 2010 at 2:34 AM
Subject: AutoReply: Out of the Office

Esteemed Correspondent:

My travels in the Andes having been prolonged unexpectedly, I'm
out of the office until the end of June, and so will be unable to check
email as frequently as I'd like. Should you have already received my
AutoReply of April, indicating a return date of mid-May (or my
earlier messages of November and/or February), *lo siento* for the
delay. In any case, please know that I value your correspondence
and look forward to responding speedily upon my return.

    Actually, can I make a confession? I had promised myself, when
I signed into my inbox, to update this message quickly and then to

return my literary *magnum opus*, but I've now spent the last hour futzing with the above paragraph, trying to counterfeit the authentically breezy tone of a man with better things to do, and since every improvement in the counterfeiting only carries me further away from anything genuine, it occurs to me that the only route out of the psychic weeds is that of full disclosure. So here goes: This entire series of AutoReplies is a well-intentioned lie that has spun out of control. I'm not really in Peru, nor have I been at any point this year or any other. The Spanish above appears courtesy of Google Translate. In fact, I don't actually have an office to be out of, unless you count a futon next to my son's overfull diaper pail, in which case, contrary to my representations, I am very much in the office. Another misrepresentation: I don't like to check email "frequently" at all. But as the machine on which I'm composing the *magnum opus*—the machine on which you may one day read it, assuming I ever finish work on this AutoReply and get back to real writing—is also the machine that brings me my email, it requires all manner of connivance to stay away.

Indeed, it's this shortening of the distance between writer and audience, between desktop and marketplace, that kept sucking me back into the inbox in the first place, occasioning some magnum delays with the novel. If I'm being completely honest, I logged in an hour ago—well, two now, really—not so much to update this message, which after all could have waited until tomorrow, but for the very same reason that I always log in. That is: I half-expected to find the email I've been waiting for all these years, the one that says that I've been discovered, that someone wants to give me a half-million dollars and a 4,000-word profile in the *New York Times Magazine*, and that my years in the wilderness are over. This is an exaggeration, but only slightly (he wrote, with what he hoped was winning candor).

Instead, what typically awaits in my inbox is a rejection notice, or a link to a *New York Times Magazine* profile of some other, more accomplished thirty-year-old. And I'm only a click away from Amazon, whose sales rankings offer a handy index of how deep in the wilderness one truly is. By the time I return to actual writing, I'm seeing every sentence through the eyes of a disembodied third party with a five-star rating system and an ax to grind. The *magnum opus* is not funny enough, or is too funny. It needs fewer adverbs, or more. It needs to be written by Junot Díaz, rather than myself. I've always thought that the aesthetic choices of a great artist should arise from imperatives in the work itself, but once I'm out here, dissolved in the masses, I can't even hear those imperatives anymore. I can't even hear myself think.

I should probably revise the above paragraph, in which I see I used the word "I" eight times. I've already done it four—well, five—in this one. Which is another, paradoxical, component of my email allergy. Even as email brings me into messy proximity with imaginary Others, it somehow encourages me to imagine those Others thinking almost exclusively about ME. It promotes the kind of self-conscious self-involvement that leads to, for example, the conceit that anyone might still be reading an Out-of-Office reply after 700 recursive words. That is, it leads me to lose track of you, Esteemed Correspondent, as the kind of independent reader I'd hoped the *magnum opus* would be worthy of.

It's entirely possible that this says more about my own anxious, superstitious, and miswired mind than about the technology itself (though "anxious, superstitious, and miswired" seems a fair descriptor of most fiction writers I know). But it sits uneasily against my sense that writing should be an act of empathy. The writers who are my heroes have always cultivated a distinctive brand of anonymity—of silence, cunning, and exile. I want to be seated halfway down the dinner table, like Henry James, ears open for the anecdote in which the lives of others suddenly blaze up before me. But how can I be a person on whom nothing is lost when I'm the only one in the room?

Finally, and perhaps most toxically for my writing life, email—the catalyst for so much tension—seems even now to offer an escape from it. To sit down at the writing desk each morning is to confront the white whale, the nothing that makes no secret of itself. The joy of fiction is a joy that lies on the far side of that *angst*. But how easy it seems, when the going gets tough, to click over to email . . . and from there to enter the comparatively hedonic bottomlessness of the internet. I start out writing a scene; I end up watching Colbert. At this rate, I'll never finish the book.

Here is something Don DeLillo said in his *Paris Review* interview:

> Words on a page, that's all it takes to help [the writer] separate himself from the forces around him, streets and people and pressures and feelings. He learns to think about these things, to ride his own sentences into new perceptions.

There's been a lot of talk lately about how the transformation of that "page"—the migration of texts from paper to screens—will transform the practice of literature. But the fact is that, through the word processor and the web browser, the migration is already well underway. And insofar as we accept DeLillo's premise that the writer needs critical distance from the forces around him, the digitization of his tools has been no help at all.

That's not to say that email hasn't made life beyond the desk more convenient and efficient. For writers, it can be a point of connection with the republic of letters and an avenue to freelancing checks without end. But it also promotes, at least in your correspondent, the same strange admixture of commodification, narcissism, and inertia that seems hardwired into each new marvel of information technology: the cell phone, the webcam, the Facebook wall. We might ask ourselves if it will be somehow encoded in the e-book, particularly on devices that also allow us to watch movies and Skype and skim the newspaper while we mean to be reading *The Magic Mountain*.

Then again, one doesn't imagine good writing has ever been easy. Maybe difficulty is even necessary, somehow. And so, after signing off here, I'm going to try once again to be "Out of the Office," but only in order to be more fully in it, on the green slopes of fiction, in the Peru of the mind. It's unclear how long the trip will take. But in the meantime, please know that I am doing my best really to think of you—the actual *you*, the Esteemed Correspondent, the independent reader, whom I do genuinely value. And that I look forward to returning.

Yours,
&c. &c.
–sent from my iPad–

IN THE CORPOREAL AGE, WE WILL KNOW THE NAMES OF TREES

Sonya Chung

It's dangerous to predict the future; I don't go in for it much. Today is all we have and all we know, I always say. This philosophy perhaps comes with age. I used to fret over the future a lot: I made plans; I saved up (money and other kinds of capital—emotional and creative, for instance); I assumed things about who I'd be and what I'd be doing and with whom I'd be doing it, *x* or *xx* years down the road. Considering the future is nothing terrible in itself; it's just when those considerations begin outweighing the present, the here and now, that you get into trouble. You start arranging, and projecting, and spending your energy on either making it so (if your predictions are desirable ones) or twisting about in avoidance (if they are not). You begin living by fear—of what will or will not happen.

That said, we can still speak in terms of *hopes*, can't we? Cornel West has said (my paraphrase) that hope is not the same as optimism. Optimism says, "Things will get better." Hope is what we exercise in spite of our knowledge that things may not get better.

The future of books, the book world, and the role of the writer is our topic. Predictions abound because we're in such a wacky moment, a hyperflux-y moment. Art, commerce, and technology are colliding like so many boiling-point particles. All the players are scrambling to survive, to thrive, to stay ahead of the (hairpin) curve. As a writer, it would be easy to fall into all that arranging and projecting and twisting about; it could also be fatal.

In 2010, I consider myself neither young nor old, so it's particularly important for me, I suppose, to both embrace realism and willfully lean toward hope. So: What might we imagine to be around that bend, realistically? And how might we hope to respond?

As we consider the future of books—the creation, distribution, and consumption thereof—we are considering, I think, questions of human behavior in a changing environment. Meaning, all debates about the evolution of books and book culture are, at heart, debates about human nature. What do we, as readers and writers, need, desire, fear, value; and how will these manifest in our choices and behavior as we accelerate further into the digital age?

Realistically: the printed book, in hardcover at the least, may well go by the wayside. By all accounts, digital technologies and the market are pushing print, as we know it, to the margins. Along with this, the prospect of making a living as a writer is dwindling; what can be got for free will not be paid for, and while commercial players will surely reorient to identify and exploit alternative income streams, the writer—my guess—will be the first to be edged out from whatever miniscule monetary rewards he managed to eke out in the first place. And surprisingly (to me), many reader-consumers are content to go along for the digital ride; bytes of literature are evidently as good as pages, especially if the price point for a new release drops as a result.

The writer will thus increasingly find that his primary talents, energies, and time will pour into work for which he will not be compensated; he will divert more and more time and energy toward non-writing work, which earns a living. For some, this may be just fine—that teaching job, or advertising job, or arts administration job is not so bad, the humble writer might say or think; merely the cost of doing business; to write is a privilege at any rate. (Some authors may begin earning their primary living via "personal connection" opportunities, such as speaking engagements—writing-related, perhaps, and yet for many authors the furthest cry from writing.) An attitude of wistful resignation will set in, a deep-sighing acceptance of this state of affairs, perhaps an occasional harkening back to a warmer, more vibrant time in cultural-literary life, when the work of the writer was revered just a little, and valued, materially.

All this may well be the reality of the moment. There is little, thus, about which the writer may be optimistic, materially speaking.

My *hope*, on the other hand, is that the above trajectory is not a foregone conclusion; or if it is, not a permanent one. I return to basic questions of human nature. Is it possible that human nature has undergone a sky-scraping pendulum swing toward the immaterial, toward hyper-volume and hyper-plurality, toward breadth over depth, multi-tasking over focus, lateral over vertical, mobility over fidelity, speed over slowness; and that soon we'll be swinging back (if we have not already begun doing so)?

We are swinging wide and high, and have been doing so for some time. There is euphoria about this for some, a sense of infinite possibility, gates thrown open for writers and readers alike: The hyperlink is the golden key, the silver bullet, one click to the publisher's cash-in, or the writer's fame, or the reader's emotional-intellectual fulfillment. But there is also discomfort, overload, disorientation. Too much of a good thing. Wading in shallow pools of generalism, gorging our information and infinite-selection appetites to soul-sickness.

Pendulum swings of this kind seem to accompany major advances in culture and civilization. The analogy that comes to mind is the evolution of feminism. Women (middle-class women, I should say) are professional peers to men, leaders in every sector, married and unmarried, straight and gay; they are, in a word, Out. But now that they are Out, they are struggling also to get back In—to be true to their bodies, which for many means both the joys and physical demands of motherhood, hearth-and-home for the twenty-first century. Women have been on the pendulum swing toward professional and intellectual achievement, and they are swinging back. They are reclaiming the corporeal: soul equals mind *and* body.

The analogy extends. The digital age has flung us Out of our bodies. I think—I hope, the way Dr. West exhorts us to hope—that we're going to want back In. That the Information Age will give way to the Corporeal Age.

In the Corporeal Age, an e-book will seem like astronaut food, or a Slim-Fast diet. And a Facebook "friend" will smack of Kubrik-esque creepiness, with all the porousness and self-revelation of social networking eventually striking our children, and children's children, as bizarrely dysfunctional; where were our boundaries? We'll resurrect *Dirty Dancing* as a cult classic—again, finding our way back into our bodies en route to soul-wellness—and embrace the mantra given to us by the late Patrick Swayze: "This is my dance space, this is your dance space."

Mobility will grow tiresome; we'll want to stay put and re-discover what it means to have roots—longevity, fidelity to place. We'll hold down jobs for longer, stop packing up and moving to a different neighborhood, apartment, city, every 2.5 years. We'll acquire heavy, solid-wood bookshelves that do not disassemble with an Allen wrench and won't be thinking, when considering buying a printed book, that we'll have to box and haul these in a year or two. Our two-week or three-month "breaks" from Facebook—"Need to detox! Back in a bit!"—will extend indefinitely. We'll go for long walks (not on treadmills), we'll rekindle our romance with the land, we'll garden and keep goats and chickens, and we'll know, as Nabokov is said to have insisted for aspiring writers, the names (and perhaps even the scents) of trees. We'll chew on less information more deeply, and laugh at how we once thought everything was knowable as long as we sat at our computers and i-devices, acquiring more and more information, apps, favorites, blogrolls.

Those of us who write will write better books. We'll pare back on blog-blabbing, will be freer from self-consciousness, quieter in our heads, slower and less distracted, more imaginatively limber and inventive.

Those of us who read will read more books. We'll pare back on blog-surfing, will be quieter in our heads, slower and less distracted, more imaginatively limber and inventive.

None of this is true prediction; prediction is backed by gobs of information, of data. For me, it's more a feeling in the air, a feeling of potential—energy gathered up into the pendulum at its apex, suspended and replete. It's a what-goes-up-must-come-down-one-way-or-another kind of feeling. In that sense, whether you are optimistic or pessimistic, hopeful or dispirited, it is clear that our needs, desires, fears, and values are at stake; and what could be more exciting for literature?

FINALLYFAST.COM AND PLAYING THE BOOK

Ander Monson

I don't know about you, but I find myself wanting to participate more and more often in the media I consume. Wait, I don't just consume that media. I muck around in it. I DVR it. I PDF it. I MP3 it. I collage it. I save it. I download it. I pirate it. I transcribe it. I quote it. I own it. I surround myself with it. Find myself in it. If I look long enough at it I begin to think I am it, iPod playlist golem, Amazon golem, iPad golem, experimental novel golem, chapbook golem.

This happens with music most obviously. I want it fast and loud and oh! and now. I want to use it to soundtrack my now. To understand my now. To remake my mood, my approach to now. To make some memories. I want to make virtual (or actual) mix tapes, playlists, and share them with others. I want to remix it, to mash it up. To *Rock Band* it up. To *Guitar Hero* it up. To sing the hell out of some karaoke. To air guitar it up. To make crazy, crappy YouTube videos of myself dancing or singing or fucking or miming to the songs I love.

Wait. I'm not talking about me; I'm talking about us. And music's not the only locus of this playfulness. We television and film viewers have been getting more involved with our media too. On the internet you can find a ton of different unofficial amateur edits of the *Star Wars* prequels. You can find a homemade trailer for *The Shining* reconceptualizing it as an uplifting family film. You can find the news, Auto-Tuned, remixed by hipsters.

My favorite iteration of this participatory instinct is the user response to a particularly wack late-night TV commercial for the website FinallyFast.com that promises to clear your Internet Explorer caches, clean your machine of spyware, tune it up, slick it up, speed it up.

If you find yourself watching a lot of late night cable like I do, then you know what I'm talking about. Lines like "My computer used to be fast. Really fast. But now it's only kinda fast . . ." and "Mom! The internet is *so slow*!!" are delivered woodenly by stock photo actors in a way that would seem to be a mockery of a commercial. The badness is wonderful. My wife and I mouth the lines in tandem sunk down on the couch. Either we possess it or it possesses us; I'm not sure which.

I checked YouTube, checked Wikipedia, because that's what you do when you watch television nostalgically on the sectional. On YouTube I found dozens of amateur remakes of the FinallyFast.com commercial. By the time this is published there may be hundreds. The ease of making and manipulating video has opened the door to us amateur fan-filmmakers. We are bored. We are drunk. We like to show it off, to shake it for the masturbators on Chatroulette. We like to mock things, to make things, to shock things into understanding, as long as we can share what we (re)make with others.

Same goes for video games, MMPORPGs, and other online communities. We like to get involved. We like to *play*. Which is a way of saying that all these things—like much in our lives (Weight Watchers, anyone? Collecting credit card miles and points, anyone? Doritos: The Quest, anyone?) are becoming more gamelike and plastic, easily manipulated.

I think I know what this means for the film, the television show, the commercial, the song, the video, the video game, the album, the EP. The sorts of media and media-makers that make or find or at least tacitly allow space for audience participation are going to get more viewers, listeners, and gamers involved in their collective meaning-making.

But what does this mean for the book? The writer? It seems we are concerned. We should be. But we're concerned about the wrong things.

The book—the *story* in particular, more than film, more than music—has always been a participatory medium. Recent studies of reading suggest that the brain exhibits the same activity when reading as it does in a real life experience, so that in some sense reading is not just simulation but *experience*, which we as readers participate in with whatever we bring to the table already. But there are more obvious ways in which we participate in books, in stories. Take for instance book clubs, *Harry Potter* parties, author readings and signings. The promised and never-really-delivered hypertext revolution. The enjoyable witch hunts that follow the publication of increasingly outlandish fake memoirs that we insist on believing in until we don't. Take the tourist attraction of Emily Dickinson's home. The invention of the LongPen, Margaret Atwood's telesigning robot hand.

It should be obvious by now that many readers, particularly younger readers—we giggling younger readers—want to find ways of interacting with stories. We want to inhabit them, consume them. We want to change them, add to them, expand and continue to populate their universe. We want to *play* them. We want to be ourselves in them. We want to make ourselves over through them. Take for instance the collaborative mass fiction of *Dungeons & Dragons*. Take for instance MUDs (Multi-User Dungeons). Take for instance *House of Leaves*. Take for instance fan fiction.

I wouldn't worry about the future of story. Story is inescapable. We can't *not* perceive our lives as stories, even if we know that stories—even the ones we tell ourselves about who we are—are fiction. That's how the brain works. In this dissolving, data-fragmented world, we all desire narrative (as opposed to the actual lived experience of unsatisfying fragments, random encounters, and passing glances). We will continue to consume it. And we will continue to create it. And if this means we need to redefine the definition of *writer*, that's okay with me. If we are all participating, then we are all writers, contributors, content-creators, storytellers. We live in an increasingly simulated, mediated world where we want to interact with stories, where we all imagine we have our own stories to tell. We tell ourselves these stories every day. Isn't that what memory is for? What Facebook is for? Twitter? Our blogs? Tumblrs? Flickr photo streams? Our comment threads? Our instant messaging? Our course evaluations? We like story—we like making stories—a lot. We like *I* a lot, like to talk about our experiences a lot. We say *like* a lot, too. The ascendancy of the memoir, the genre of *I* and of the moment, cashes in on this desire.

I know only a few of us who call ourselves writers who are excited about these developments. Some of us are worried. Some of us know we're supposed to be worried about our dwindling advances, but we don't care. We can't imagine not reading and writing books. But we should be excited. Writers have been stuck in that old technology, that old but shockingly good technology of the codex, for a long time. Maybe that's our problem, that we've relaxed too much into the ease of the form. We've taken it for granted. Many of us grew up only knowing composition on word processing programs, never even feeling the physical mechanism of the carriage return which still gives that *return* key on the keyboard its anachronistic name. We never felt the physical exertion that typing on a manual typewriter required. We never handwrote after grade school exercises in learning cursive.

What I'm saying is that we've forgotten how it can *feel* to *make* a book. I don't mean just how it feels to *write* a book, but how it feels to *make one*. Our experience with the codex has been so long and lately mediated—through programs like Microsoft Word in which we are able to produce—process—virtual words on virtual pages with virtual drop shadows suggesting the depth of a physical page, which are then saved in ones and zeroes encoded magnetically or optically on hard drives or flash media. We would do well to reconnect with what books feel like in the hands, what they smell like, what the pages sound like when they flex, friction, and turn, what they are or can be. We've allowed our publishers to do the thinking about a lot of this. We've let our editors do the editing, our word processors the word processing, the designers the designing, production managers the production, the marketers the marketing, the eight maids a-milking the milking. And so on.

The bad news is that many, if not all, of these roles are reverting back to writers. The good news is that a lot of these formerly forbidden spaces are opening up to writers. We would be wise to remember that we writers are first *makers*. That we can make paper—any size we like, not just the 8.5" x 11" American default "letter size"—out of wood pulp. That we can hand-mix our inks. That we can physically letterpress those inks into that paper and feel the physical impression. That we can hand-bind and stitch. That we can photocopy. Cut the pages how we like. Handprint on whatever part of the book we like. That we can do whatever we want with design. That we aren't stuck with the default margins, the double-spacing, the Times New Roman, the Lulu or iUniverse presets. The standard English. The standard syntax. The realist, prose-transparent third-person stories featuring timely epiphanies. The autocapitalized first letters of sentences, or lines. The autocorrected grammar. The sort of narrative or lyric in style at the time.

These defaults, these shortcuts are useful. They save time. They reduce the number of variables. They speak to certain readerships. They are required by some standard book formats, convenient technologies of printing and binding and distribution. We are after all in a world of near-paralyzing capability. But if they go unexamined, if we think our only job as writers is to write nice sentences and hand them off to someone else, we risk obsolescence or, at the least, irrelevance.

If we expect readers to participate in our texts, our sentences, our lines, our books (or our e-books), we must participate more fully in the making of our books. We must make space for them to participate in the physical artifact of the book, to think about its form, the pacing of the page turning, the leading between lines, the smell of the paper, to understand why this book, this object, is the best form to experience and participate in the story we're telling.

The job of future writers is to hack into any available space, to test the limits of the system, to think about the variables, to challenge their own assumptions and the assumptions of others. Are writers going to be marginalized? We already have been. We always have been. We need to inhabit the margin, to be on the edge of a culture, a place, a story. It's the best vantage point to see it anew. This has always been the job of the artist—not just to repeat the received wisdom about whatever world is in question but to make and push and test whatever boundaries we can find. Some of those boundaries are going to be increasingly technological. Just recently, Apple announced that individual writers are now allowed to publish and distribute electronic texts in its iBookstore app.

Of course that will come with constraints, what we're told we're allowed to do. But constraints are good, and they are not absolute. Form creates tension, and we want tension, elasticity, electricity.

So for the writer willing to play with and look seriously at her own medium (or media), the news is good. Are we going to have to find new ways to get noticed? Yes. Do we *get* to find new ways to get noticed? Yes. Is it trouble? Yes. But trouble is the stuff of writing and creation. Time to shut up and get to the making, get back to that sense of play where everything interesting, including the future, finally fast and soon to be here, starts.

SCRIBBLE

Victor LaValle

When I was twenty-four I attended a party thrown by one of the most fabulous students in my writing program. The apartment was on the Upper East Side, and I was living out at the ass-end of Queens; I'd moved back home with my family to save money during grad school. I traveled all that way to the party because I wanted to sleep with this woman, the host. That was never actually going to happen, I understood this even then, but I'm kind of a stubborn bastard so I decided to try anyway. The worst that would happen was that she'd say no, and I could live with that.

So I reached the place and one thought occurred to me as soon as I stepped inside: How does a graduate student afford a place like this? A two-bedroom apartment somewhere in the east nineties cost more than a little something, whether rented or owned. And this wasn't some run-down spot. Exposed brick walls in the living room, a small kitchen appointed with every gadget one might need to prepare dinner for a diplomat. Two bedrooms. A bathroom with separate shower and tub. When I stepped inside I tried to guess how I should act in such an environment. I thought back on all my experiences with the moneyed classes. This had consisted mostly of repeated viewings of *Trading Places* over the years. Unfortunately, I felt pretty sure I wasn't playing the Eddie Murphy role. Maybe I was that waiter who got a bad tip from the Duke brothers.

I'm being silly, of course. No one treated me like a servant. Everyone was cool with me. I had lots of friends in the place. The distinction that mattered most that night had to do with our genres. (A ridiculous sentence to have to type, I agree.) The poets floated with the poets, the fiction writers huddled together in clumps, the non-fiction writers commandeered the kitchen. And I did my best to snag a little time with the woman I'd come to see, but she didn't have much time to give. She was our host, and she enjoyed the role. She was good at it, too. Somehow, she was always the person who greeted each new guest at the door. If she had to sprint from the bathroom, hurdle over ten novelists in a single bound, she would do it just to be sure that her grin was the first one you saw. But as soon as you walked in the door, got your kiss and hug, the lady got *gone.*

I heard her voice more often than I saw her face. I'd stroll into the kitchen because I'd heard her discussing some current events with the non-fiction writers, but no sooner had I arrived than she'd moved on to the poets, and she stood with them whispering mystically. No sooner had I maneuvered around to the poets than she'd flitted on to the fiction writers who were all grumbling about something, how they'd been overlooked, short-changed, or cheated. And I was left standing there with the poets, who weren't exactly unfriendly; they were very tolerant of my presence, but as soon as I left the group they returned to guzzling cocktails while they gently flapped their vellum-thin wings. And by the time I reached the fiction writers? New guests were at the door, enjoying her attentions.

This went on all night. It wasn't that she was giving me the brush-off, I felt confident—even then—that she enjoyed my company just fine. But just. Plus her boyfriend was at the party. He wasn't a writer. I don't know what he did. I remember he spoke some European language fluently. He wore open-toed sandals—a grown man!—but still managed to seem elegant. I had to give him points for that.

By the end of the evening I'd figured out that she and I were not to be. And once I'd stopped acting goony over her, I was able to enjoy the party. These guests were friends of mine, and living two hours away from upper Manhattan meant that I never saw them outside of classes. So why not enjoy this night? Soon enough I'd found a nice place right near the bookshelves in the living room; they ran the length of a whole wall. All hardcovers.

In my home, growing up, we'd had one tiny bookshelf that carried the entire Encyclopedia Brittanica series. That was our "library." And we only had those because my mother had been convinced by a fifth grade teacher that my sister and I would need them for book reports. Which had been true. I'd copy entries verbatim, show my completed homework to my mother, and then I was free to go outside all evening and play.

The books that I called my own, since I was a bookish kid by nature, were cheap paperbacks that rarely survived for more than a few weeks. I'd read them in bed and crush pages in my sleep or just lose them somewhere between school and home. If I got bored in class I'd doodle faces in the margins, or tear off a back cover so I could write a note to one of my boys on the blank space inside. I loved to read, but books were disposable. So to see all these hardbacks together, running in rows along the living room wall, well, I was more impressed by this than by the apartment. They made up one fine looking library.

And, suddenly, here she was; my host. She'd seen me pawing at her books and just had to come over. We spent the next ten minutes picking one book or another off the shelf. If anyone new arrived at the door it seemed like she ignored them. She just had to show me this one, both for the cover design and to see if I'd read the author. Then on to the next. Just plucking them down and leafing through the pages, admiring the sentences or the sans-serif.

She pulled down a book by William Vollmann. *Butterfly Stories.* I'd read *Whores for Gloria* and *An Afghanistan Picture Show* and felt like devouring more. She put the book in my hand and I read the first sentence of Vollmann's brief introduction to the novel. "In case any of you readers happens to be a member of the Public, that mysterious organization that rules the world through shadow-terrors . . ." Good enough for me!

I shut the book. "Can I borrow this?"

She smiled and put her hand on my shoulder—so nice!—and said, "No."

I almost dropped the book. It bobbled between my hands so she grabbed it from me and slipped it back onto the shelf, right where it had been before.

"I don't lend my books out," she said. "I can't. They always used to come back, *if* they came back, with stains or bent pages, or even someone's little ink stains in the margins! I decided, years ago, that I would never let them out of my sight again. I'm sorry."

Poof, that was it. She left for the kitchen or the front door or the moon. And I stood there for minutes. Actual minutes. Waiting for her to return, laugh, slip the book off the shelf and hand it to me. But she never did. My disappointment burned my face, like shame, but it wasn't just the rejection. I was also stunned that this person I liked, and respected as a writer, would treat her books this way. As if the objects themselves were, somehow, as valuable as the words and ideas they contained.

My wife and I live in a two-bedroom apartment in Washington Heights. We've turned the back room into a den for us and an office for me. She uses a portion of our living room as her office space. We keep all our books in the back, where I work. Right now we've got a few very tall bookshelves and they're jammed with paperbacks and hardcovers. Not as neatly lined up as the ones in that East Side apartment, but I'm always happy when I walk into the room and see them there.

If you pull down the books that are mine, meaning the ones I brought with me from my single life, you can open more than half and find handwritten notes, sometimes whole paragraphs, scribbled on the end pages, or in the margins of the text. I've got a copy of *Butterfly Stories*, in hardcover, and when I opened the back cover while working on this essay I found one word written at the bottom of the very last page of the story. I wrote, "Yikes!"

Other books offer (slightly) more scintillating commentary. In them you'll find lines that are trial runs for stuff in my own fiction. Something in a certain book just smacked me with inspiration and I needed to write an idea down. Why not right there in the book I'm holding? Because I do this so regularly, a vast number of my books are unsellable, but they sure are valuable to me.

So when people discuss the future of the book, how readers and writers and editors and bookstores might actually make peace with the electronic book (and maybe even embrace it), I tend to think of my little notes. Can I underscore some text on an electronic reader? Or write a note to myself after reading something invigorating in *Toni Cade Bambara*? Right now, from all the reports, the answer is yes, but the effects are dodgy. I can't imagine that'll last long.

When earlier e-readers came out, I felt underwhelmed mostly because the pages all looked like dot-matrix print. But in just a few years they've managed to render a fairly stylized looking "page." How much longer before a reader can use her finger to highlight a passage reliably, or pull up a little keyboard display that allows her to insert her sudden revelation right alongside Barry Hannah's prose? She could hide or show these comments like when using "track changes" in Word.

And once those possibilities seem imminent, it becomes easy to imagine even greater power in the reader's hands. Eventually, maybe even the ability to revise the text as the reader sees fit. Why not? I'm guessing this sounds damn near blasphemous to some folks, but a master file, the original novel, could always remain. I could just make a copy and *tinker*. Honestly, how would my removing all Levin's farming scenes from *Anna Karenina* do any harm to Tolstoy? Leo's ghost won't rise and take revenge! The only one who'd be altered by this act is me. And maybe my destructive act would actually serve to educate. I never appreciate how expertly a machine works until I've taken it apart. The best future I can imagine for the novel is one where the book is cherished a little less. The two aren't the same thing, after all.

Now let me be clear: If you've got an original copy of William Blake's *Illustrations of the Book of Job*, please don't write in the margins and please don't think any e-book is going to compare. But, let's be honest, you don't have that shit. (If you do, let me hold it for a minute?) Most of the books on your bookshelves might be beautifully designed, and not exactly cheap, but they're no more divine than a toaster. They are mass-produced items, sold in (occasionally) mass quantities. So what, exactly, makes them so dear?

It's not the book, but the *idea* of the book. Some man or woman spent weeks or months or years or a lifetime *bleeding* on the page! Now you hold that essence in your hands! And other melodramatic nonsense. It all strikes me as a pretty Old Testament way of thinking. Treating a book like a pair of stone tablets. A series of commandments, inviolable, handed down by a deity. (Though, let's clarify something folks, writers ain't Yahweh.) I think we writers like it when books are treated this way because we get to enjoy the reflected glory, even if it's just at modestly attended conferences. Very few of us are ever going to get wealthy from this stuff, so we might as well be honored, right?

But I have to admit, I'm more of a New Testament guy. I'm thinking here of the Gospels of Matthew, Mark, Luke, and John. Four books that, many scholars agree, were written, rewritten, and then edited long after the events they narrate took place. And those stories were told and retold, reshaped, for decades before any of it was written down definitively. Would this be such a terrible fate for the book? I don't think so. The greatest gift the electronic age could bestow upon the novel is to keep it sacred, not sacrosanct.

THE CHAMELEON MACHINE

Emily St. John Mandel

1.

There are certain divisions in the world that seem unnecessary to me. Consider, for a moment, the e-book/paper book divide. On the one side, the traditionalists, with their—okay, *our*—love of the objects that we call books. The texture of the paper, the beautiful dust jackets. Being able to see how much of a book remains to be read, as pages stack up on the left and diminish on the right. The ability to see two pages at once and have a sense of what's coming. Writing in the margins.

On the other side stand the gadgeteers with their cold slim readers, packing entire libraries into a volume the size of a novella, flipping pages on a touchscreen. I don't own a digital reader, but I understand why other people do. Aside from the natural joy of owning a shiny new gadget, there's an undeniable appeal from a purely minimalist standpoint—why agonize over which two books to cram into your suitcase, when you can bring your entire library with you?—and I have to imagine that e-book aficionados have a much easier time of moving than I do. When I move to a new apartment, it's a Herculean task involving towering mountains of extremely heavy small boxes with labels like *Fiction: Ames–Bellow* and *Theater Books: Box 1 of 10.* It isn't pretty.

Digital readers and paper books have little in common. But both objects have considerable merit, and this is why I think we should combine the two.

The future of the book that I imagine involves an object that looks, in every detail, like a high-quality hardcover. The difference is that there's no title visible on either the cover or the spine. When you first open the book, all the pages are blank. Hundreds of pages of high-quality paper—a slight sheen might hint at the underlying circuitry—with nothing on them. The cover is blank too.

You might mistake the object for a blank notebook, except for the discreet touchscreen on the inside of the front cover. Here you scroll through your library, and select the book you want to read. For old time's sake, let's say *The Catcher in the Rye.* Once you've made your selection, the pages remain blank for just a heartbeat—the process taking place in the heart of the book's machinery is, after all, quite complex—but then the famous orange carousel horse of the first edition dust jacket rises slowly out of the blankness of the front cover, like an image rising out of Polaroid film. JD Salinger appears on the spine above the publisher's logo, and then all at once the pages begin to fill. The book is typesetting itself.

The first page is no longer blank. Beneath the Chapter One heading, the famous and incorrigible opener has appeared: "If you really want to hear about it, the first thing you'll probably want to know is where I was born . . ."

The object in your hands looks and feels like a book. The pages feel like paper. You flip through them, and all the words are there waiting for you; there's no waiting for a screen to refresh. The object might even be made, with a judicious dash of library-scented accord from your favorite perfume shop, to smell like the books you grew up with. You can make notes on the pages if you wish, provided you use the special digital pen attached by means of a thin ribbon to the spine.

But suppose you get tired of reading Salinger after awhile, or you finish the book. You go back to your touchscreen just inside the front cover, and flip through your library until you find something that appeals to you. Select the new volume, and the process begins again. Just a moment of blankness, while Salinger's carousel horse fades out. The notes you took in the margins have vanished, but they'll be there again the next time you want to read *The Catcher in the Rye*.

And then Leo Tolstoy is on the spine. Turn the first page and the text of Salinger's book has dissolved. The first line of the novel now reads as follows: "Happy families are all alike; every unhappy family is unhappy in its own way."

The book in your hands is now *Anna Karenina*.

2.

It only sounds like magic. Electronic paper—flexible sheets of paper-like material, comprised in various versions of polymer, microcapsules of oil, arrays of electrodes—has been around since the '70s, when Nick Shelton at Xerox's Palo Alto Research Center created the first sheet of the stuff. Research continued in the decades that followed, and in early 2010 LG debuted a new prototype: a sheet of electronic paper with the dimensions of a newspaper page, weighing only 130 grams.

In the photographs that accompanied the press release, the material has a glassy patina; a man and a woman hold sheets of LG's new paper in what looks like the Tokyo subway system, and the sheets display the front page of a daily newspaper. It doesn't quite look like paper, but it's close. It's so close.

Is there any reason why, a few years from now, when the technology's become lighter and better and less expensive, we couldn't make entire books out of this stuff? There are of course logistical problems to consider—how to manage the display of a 600-page novel on a device that only has 350 pages, for instance— but this sort of thing doesn't strike me as being particularly insurmountable.

It seems to me that the failing of our digital readers to date is that the focus has been purely on the *content*. Our earliest books were sublimely executed works of art, years and decades and entire lifetimes poured into the lettering and ornamentation of medieval manuscripts. The printing press changed all of this, of course, but the ghost of that early obsession with beauty has lingered. Beautiful books have remained with us, in ever-changing form, through all the seasons of publishing: gorgeous book jackets, impeccably designed interiors, gilt lettering on cloth. But digital readers have been focused solely on finding the best possible means of presenting the book's words, of inventing the ideal flatscreen to display them on. I fear we're nearing a point of forgetting the idea of books as objects, as works of art whose *form,* not just whose content, we might consider preserving.

3.

The book in your hands has transformed itself into *Anna Karenina*, but why stop there? One of the major problems of reading is the difficulty of ignoring the chaotic world around you. We've all been stuck in airplanes with screaming small children. Because blocking out this sort of thing by sheer willpower alone can be impossible, I wonder if perhaps our books might be enlisted to help us out.

I read a fascinating article a few years back about directed-sound technology and its potential for in use in museums. One of the aural problems of museums is that some patrons want to hear information about what they're standing in front of, whereas others would vastly prefer to contemplate in silence. The idea with the directed-sound technology is that if you'd like to learn more about a particular display, you step into a specific location in the room—perhaps indicated by a circle of light projected onto the floor—and there, only *there*, at that particular point, in a discretely projected column of ultrasonic sound, you hear a recorded voice explaining the nuances of sixteenth-century Chinese calligraphy or the finer details of the Battle of Brooklyn.

Directed-sound technology has advanced to the point that beams of sound can be directed at individuals in such a way that the people sitting on either side of them will hear nothing. All of this makes me think that the book, once the technology advances a little further and can be easily embedded without adding too much weight, should have a noise-canceling button. Click it and step into the circle of light; you'd be cast, all at once, into your own private aural landscape. Perhaps it might enable silence, or some sort of soothing ambient noise. Care would have to be taken not to zone out completely at, say, airport departure gates, but I think the concept has promise.

I was thinking the other day of sound-enabled picture books. It would be a strange and dazzling new form. Page upon page of gorgeous illustrations, with music, with text and spoken word that no one but the reader could hear. An interactive art project. Or imagine the more practical applications for travel books: On the page listing useful phrases for the country you're traveling in, you could hear the pronunciation before you spoke, so as to avoid making a fool of yourself when you're trying to order coffee in Slovakia.

4.

For all my love of the electronic innovations of the late twentieth and early twenty-first centuries, there are certain tactile experiences that I'm not willing to surrender. The experience of turning pages is one of them. I love machines, but I want the book I hold in my hands fifty years from now to look like the books I remember from childhood. I want to be able to see two pages at a time, I want to take notes in the margins, I want to flip backward to see what I missed. Most importantly, I want the bookstores I love to continue to exist in the future.

The conveniences of the digital age are inarguable. I've never really liked grocery shopping; it's nice that now I can do it online at 2 AM. I feel the same way about buying shoes. But books? That's something else entirely. I imagine the bookstores of the future. They'd look very much like the bookstores of now, except it's possible that they might be a little smaller; if most people are downloading books to machines, they'd need much less stock. A few people might still want to buy the old kind of book, the kind made out of paper, especially at author events. Those of us with the new books, the ones made out of electronic paper that can transform into other books in our hands, will browse for a while and then perhaps, if we happen to be carrying our new books with us, pay for and download the volumes we want to buy. Or perhaps we'll buy books on a volume the size of a flash drive, to be downloaded to our new books when we get home later. And then we'll sit in parks and subways and on sofas, the same as we have since the invention of the printing press, and we'll flip through the pages of our beautiful machines.

WHY BOTHER?

Victoria Patterson

My nine-year-old son's story was chosen as one of five to be staged by a cast of actors at a school assembly. I watched with pride and affection as the actors performed his story about his struggle to get ready for school, unable to find one purple sock and one orange sock to wear, thus marking him as unique among his peers (even if his jeans cover the socks so that only he knows). The crowd of kids laughed and clapped, and I saw my son's face—he looked both embarrassed and proud. Later, I asked him what it was like to have his words performed on stage. As a writer, I was genuinely curious. His answer, given with a mixture of irritation and surprise: "They didn't do it the way I wrote it. They changed my words."

Part of the thrill of writing is getting a story on the page the way no one else can, whether it concerns a desire for mismatched socks or a conflict with larger implications. There's something inborn (or at least acquired very young) about feeling ownership, as a writer, over one's creation, and that compulsion to write—to get the story on the page the way it's meant to be written—is not contingent on outside forces. Writers need to write for instinctual reasons. There's a deep pride in the ability to string words and sentences and paragraphs together, to keep an organized mass of images moving forward, to create life on the page. Eudora Welty said that she wrote for the "it," which I take to mean the convergence of that overwhelming need to write with the fulfillment of that need—the moment when the words and sentences and paragraphs achieve a magical rhythm. John Updike described the deep and sustaining satisfactions of writing as "the sense of life quickening under your hands, of one sentence linking into another and a character developing a kind of plausibility and a kind of solidity." He believed that the excitement came from the work taking on a life of its own, and that "you need silence and patience to bring it off, and sometimes you may only *believe* it's happening. But in general, this is what you're there for. The joy of creation."

Rumor has it that the book industry is in catastrophic decline and that the future is bleak for writers—but when have writers had security? If a balanced and peaceful life is a measurement of success, writers haven't done so well. I recently read an anecdote about Theodore Dreiser. His publisher buried his novel *Sister Carrie*, having never read anything like it before. Dreiser barely sold any copies; in despair, he rented a room in Brooklyn and repositioned a chair in the center of the room, turning it various degrees and then sitting in it again, trying to align it—to get it right. He went in circles like that, over and over, until he ended up in a sanatorium. In an introductory fiction class I taught at UC Riverside, we read a plethora of authors from a fat anthology. My students kept a running tally on how the authors had died; the most common (overlapping) categories included insanity, alcoholism, drug addiction, syphilis, and suicide.

Mental health aside, Reynolds Price identified the transitory rewards of being a writer as "invitations to travel, chances to meet other writers who (whatever their neuroses) often make short-term company, possible brief freshets of money, and an odd priestly status," and that's about it. Vincent Van Gogh depicted the artist's life as one that makes him or her a perpetual outsider. The only respite, he believed, was to be "completely immersed" in his paintings. We know how that worked out for him—and we also know that he produced great art.

For writers, success can't be measured by common standards. More often than not, the better a book sells in its day, the less it is recognized and respected later; and oddly, rejection and failure can be more helpful, developing within a writer resilience born of hard-won—and very necessary—faith in his or her own work. Joyce Carol Oates said, "Writing is not a race. No one really 'wins.'" Reviewers and editors aren't all-knowing, all-seeing deities; they're subject to biases. Praise is not success. And criticism, however warranted or uncalled for, is not failure.

Writers need to sustain that unreasonable, almost supernatural faith—especially in the face of a shaky book industry, and at a time when the spread of the internet, with its glut of spastic information for quick consumption, has made it even more difficult to compete for readers. An unusual combination of qualities benefits a writer: humility, innocence, empathy, sensitivity, wonder, and surprise—along with the gall necessary to continue writing, and the persistence and stubbornness and arrogance to believe that he or she might have something to add to what's already been written, and that serious readers with long attention spans exist.

Given the lack of external and practical enticements, the drive to write—that deep inner thirst to create—is vital. Future writers probably won't get much credit, but as Joyce Cary notes, a writer "who counts on understanding and reward is a fool." No one is asking a writer to write. I don't write for the approval of family and friends; they get less of me when I write and can be disapproving. Before I was published, I had the impression that they thought I was wasting my time (and even after publication, this can feel like the general consensus). But at some point, it was as if I didn't have a choice. I had to write. So I kept writing. I imagine it's similar to getting struck by lightning. It feels arbitrary and strange.

So, over and over, like Dreiser rearranging his chair, I ask myself why I write, and some days are better than others. Art has purpose—Franz Kafka's "axe for the frozen sea inside"—which it accomplishes in its unique way, regardless of outside forces, with an appreciation and relish, and in defiance of definitions. The deeper appreciation and rewards are silent and anonymous—including how the work changes the writer, regardless of publication. How valuable an individual writer's work may be to someone in the future, the writer may never know. But the work remains intrinsic to the writer and worthy of pursuit.

Creativity is an affirming process, even as the book industry is deemed to be in the process of obsolescing. Rather than desiring success and self-preservation, I have a kind of humility and gratitude for the experience of life as a writer, and a tacit regard for the larger continuous dialogue among writers past, present, and future; and I have an affinity for great writing: the capacity to be moved by someone's words on a page, as deeply as I wish to move others, and a belief in the worth of the empathetic imagination. I brood over my work rather than the fate of the book industry.

SPARE US THE 3-D

Elizabeth Crane

Okay, listen up: The last thing I need to worry about, as an artist, is the future. If that sounds cavalier and/or simplistic, so be it. I already worry about the future plenty. Will we even have one? Will I? Will I be able to get by on Social Security after all those years when I was making nine or no dollars an hour? Will we run out of oil in my lifetime, forcing me to learn how to raise chickens and milk goats when I'm hobbling around with a walker? Will I continue to publish so I can hold onto my beloved teaching job, or will MFA programs cease to exist, what with there being no oil? *I have no idea.* So I'm the last person to have any predictions about the fate of fiction in the future. Are there any original ideas anymore? Could this question be asked about art in general? I have no idea of the answer to this, either, but I know for sure there are plenty of ideas I haven't read about yet. I know there are still original voices, and that counts for a lot for me, as a reader. If someone knocks out some sentences that make my heart expand or my head explode, I will have had a satisfying day, and I know that I have not yet read all those brilliant sentences. I know that there are many subjects I'm interested in reading about that relate to human experiences common to many of us, and many more that relate to experiences which may not seem out of the ordinary to those living them but which are nearly beyond my imagination. And that for each writer who's had those experiences, the potential is always there that the person will offer fresh insight or come up with a fresh way of stringing words together that I'm still willing and eager to read. I know that there are paintings that haven't been painted (because painting's supposed to be dead too, right?) that will shift my perspective, even just a tiny bit, when they arrive; I know that there are songs that haven't yet been sung, which will make me feel understood by people I will never know when they come on the radio, and that I will sit in the car to find out who wrote them (cursing DJs everywhere for mentioning the artist before and not after the song); I know that although it may be rare, every so often a movie will come along that will make me change my mind about something I'd previously been steadfast about in my personal dogma; and I know that on Facebook someone will post an animation that will make me feel like the world isn't the overwhelmingly evil place it seems to be, that more than one or two people out there feel the way I do about something and express it gorgeously, in a way I've never seen before. I have not yet grown bored of beauty, or uninterested in learning. I'm neither the fastest nor the slowest reader on earth, but I know that if books ceased to be written from this moment forward, there would still be plenty to keep me engaged until my future is said and done. The books in my own house that I haven't read yet—that right there could probably get me through the first few years. A few days ago I pulled *Maus*, by Art Spiegelman, down from the shelf. Halfway through the book, I had a small revelation. At one point, Vladek and Anja, Spiegelman's parents, are walking around with pig masks on to disguise their mouse/Jewish faces from the Nazis. I read several pages before I said to my husband, "Wow, I just realized that for the last few pages I was thinking that in Poland in 1944, this is what the mice/Jews did to hide from Nazis: walked around with pig masks." I take a small risk here of the reader thinking me insane or not terribly sharp, but I mention it to point out how absorbed I was in the book, how true it felt to me, that I read it not just as a metaphoric way to talk about the Holocaust, which of course I have as well, but also as the literal truth about these particular characters. Of course, *Maus* is a graphic novel, and part of my argument is that literature doesn't need embellishment, but it's what I'm reading right now. I also recently read *What Is the What*, also sitting on my own shelf, and which is, you know, a regular novel, which caused me to say *Oh my god* about every three pages and showed me a part of the world I haven't seen and knew little about. I have no doubt that there are countless books to be written that will open my heart and mind as these have.

I think the role of the writer will always be to write. I don't see fiction as needing the literary equivalent of 3-D to make it better. Certainly I understand that storytelling has evolved from pictures in caves to deckle-edged books and everything in between, and that the implication is that how we tell stories will likely evolve yet again. But this brain couldn't begin to guess what that will look like, and I don't need to work myself up over something I probably can't control. As a writer, I'm always interested in trying (key word: trying) to bring something fresh to the table, but not because I think it's necessary for the future of writing. I'm an artist. I have no choice but to keep doing what I do, no matter what happens.

THE BOOK

Deb Olin Unferth

The book is on its way out, I'm told. The age of the book is over, the great dragon is heading for the horizon, descending out of sight, dying. I'm trying to figure out what that means. The word "book" is an abstraction when used this way and could mean all kinds of things:

- The object, the book itself, the physical hardbound gadget.
- The text of the book, what's between the covers—the novel, the biography, the poem cluster.
- The book-writing skill: If there are fewer books, the set of skills (part craft, part intuitive art) required to write books will atrophy.
- The urge, the authorial drive to string and mold narratives, to pull what's in the mind out, put it into words, tell a few lies about it, meticulously arrange it, and hand it out to strangers. (And do we also fear losing a more general urge—the need to create story-like

impressions of ourselves? The need to create something that "lasts," to participate in a tradition?)

- The collective desire for the book: the audience and the hole the book fills in the chest, whatever it is that drives the reader, a quiet passive search of some sort, for meaning or connection, or a desire to be absent or "lost," or alternately, a desire to be present, connected, "engaged."
- The book community: the book clubs, the MFA programs, the publishing world, AWP.

Which of these are vanishing with "the end of the book"? Which would be the worst to lose?

With regard to the object itself, there does seem to be the danger that the bound book could go the way of other dated and diminished civil objects: matchbooks, hair curlers, drive-in movies—things that still exist, but thinly. There'll probably be fewer books in people's houses, fewer in backpacks and briefcases, fewer bookstores. And, yes, that's sad, because we like bookstores and backpacks full of books (even the drive-in movie still holds a place in our hearts), but you can't hold on to something out of sheer sentimentality—or you can, but it won't work. Besides, a lot of people never had any books in their briefcases to begin with. So in the long run I don't think it will matter much.

And perhaps what is inside the book, the text, is in a bit of danger as well. The original intended format for a novel or patch of poems was the stand-alone book, and if its format languishes, the form will languish—or transform to fit its new medium. The e-book: However the literary earthquake settles, if the e-book survives, writing for these devices will take on a distinct form. Apart from the e-book likely becoming a web-linked, 3-D, hologram, scratch-and-sniff device, the mind reads a screen differently than a printed page, so writing will adapt to best suit screen-reading.

As a fiction writer, I can imagine that structural elements, such as pacing, and micro-elements, such as sentence length, will change, for example. So the book-writing skill could also be in danger. The specific novel-writing, poem-composing skill set could recede or largely change. But it won't disappear completely. Some people will still write books no matter what, because it's hard (at least for me), and humans are bent on doing hard things, however thankless or meaningless.

As for the authorial urge and the collective desire for the book—how so many of us want badly to tell what it's like to be us, and how we seem fascinated with finding out what our comrades think about existence—those aren't going anywhere. Whatever it is that the book does for humanity, in the mysterious way that it does it, will still be done. Some people will still be driven to represent experience and search creatively for narrative meaning, and some people will prefer instead to toil away at their airplane-fixing or whatnot, unaided by the existential distraction of art.

And the book world? What about that? All the editors and agents and publicists and reviewers? What will become of those job-deserving folk? Oh, those sort are resilient. They'll find other places to do what they do, only a little differently. I wouldn't worry about them.

And the teaching of creative writing? What is the point in that? All those MFA programs? No, no, that's still a good idea. After all, schools are filled with courses that no longer pertain to anything.

Is it sad? Does it suck, this loss of the book-object, the dethroning of the craft? Well, for me it sucks, of course. I've spent so much time learning this particular craft, to the exclusion of all else. If you're going to mourn the decline of the book, mourn for people like me (and you: If you're reading this, you're likely one of those people too). Mourn for the generation before mine, and maybe mourn for some of our students who were silly enough to believe us when we said this was important, not at all like studying Byzantine art or French literature. Mourn for those involved in the transition, the several lingering generations, and for those of us who, as sappy youths, threw our chips in with the book and then became so specialized that any other life was soon beyond us. That part sucks. But in most ways it doesn't suck. Other things suck. Think of the billions of land animals born to be tortured and murdered for our culinary entertainment each year. Industrial fishing lines pull in fifty tons of sea animals per scoop. Think of deforestation. We're crushing whatever we can. The dying book feels gentle in comparison, insignificant and natural and precedented. I'm becoming outdated, so what. My friends are too, so what. Art forms evolve, and their media transform or are replaced. To me the earth looks like a holocaust: the bodies piling into the ground, the dirt filling with plastic and blood, while the only life left (us) crawls around the great graveyard, pulsing and ruining. If I'm going to forecast the future of narrative (What for? So we can look back at ourselves and laugh?), my guess is that the next great works—however they be rendered—are going to be an enormous outpouring of despair and regret for what we've done, our stupidity and selfishness. We'll be sitting in our septic tank, rubbing at the windows in hopes of glimpsing the fairyland we destroyed. We'll be scribbling with our knobs on our space-screens about the punishment we deserve, the punishment that isn't coming.

A KIND OF VAST FICTION*

David Gates and Jonathan Lethem

From: Jonathan Lethem
To: David Gates
Subject: the old transmission

Hey, David. As I was saying to my 2,472 friends the other day, these certainly are strange times in the history of the boundary between the human persons and the written words. What (if anything) is your strategy—given your life as a teacher (I'm a teacher again; this question's of more than mild interest), as a working journalist, as a witness to the digital quarantine-crumbling of all those distinctions between writer and reader, text and commentary, original and copy, private and public, book and computer, and so forth—for holding onto whatever it is we're supposed to still be holding onto, as "literary" writers? On my good days I think the old transaction, the old transmission, between a single writer and a single reader between hard covers (or "hard covers," whatever) is still thrumming along nicely, perhaps worth more than it

---

* "A Kind of Vast Fiction" was originally published in *PEN America 12: Correspondences* (Spring 2010) by PEN American Center. Reprinted with the permission of the authors.

ever was precisely because of all the signal and noise rebounding around outside. But not every day's a good day, I'll admit here, though I try to keep up a brave face. Not to tempt you into any unwilling pontification, but are you able to find any encouraging words for your students (I know mine are baffled)? Or for me? And why aren't you on Facebook?

From: David Gates
To: Jonathan Lethem
Subject: "Waldo, what are you doing out there?"

I may be slow on the uptake—no DOUBT I'm slow on the uptake—but I don't see much sign of such bafflement among my students. They seem to be writing short stories and novels, mostly of a conventionally realistic sort—though some of them have major romances with Beckett or Barthelme, which I try to foster, or with such contemporaries as Kelly Link—and hoping to see their work between hard covers. You'd think it was still 1953. Going to an MFA program these days may seem like training to become a farrier or a wheelwright, yet some of my students do manage get their books published. (I know, I know, for what THAT's worth. But what was it EVER worth? When exactly WAS that Golden Age?) Nor do I see much sign of their not knowing the difference between writer and reader, text and commentary, and so forth. I'm pretty clear on those distinctions myself, so maybe I generate a force field that repels postmodern thinking. And I say this having just read David Shields's *Reality Hunger*, which I know impressed you as it did me; it makes as strong an argument against conventional fiction as I can imagine. It's helped clarify for me why I can read so little fiction these days, and why I can't stand most of what I'm now writing myself. It doesn't, however, explain to me why fiction works for me when it works for me—not that this is an explanation I need. So yes, I do believe in "the old transaction, the old transmission," since I still experience it on good days, and see my students experiencing it. As you say, not every day's a good day, but that's a lot to expect. What else would I believe in? And why in God's name would I be on Facebook? ("Henry, what are you doing in there?" "Waldo, what are you doing out there?")

From: Jonathan Lethem
To: David Gates
Subject: a story about two writers

Yeah, well, you're calling my bluff here—the bafflement is probably my own, projected onto my students and injected into my classroom. I don't know if I'm generating exactly the reverse of "a force field that repels postmodern thinking," but I have done this and that to foster self-consciousness and anxiety regarding these matters in myself, in my stories and essays, and sometimes in my teaching. Yet I'd admit here that that's to some degree a kind of "dutiful bafflement," an obligation to the present moment, like I feel I'm meant to open my practice to the latest advances in pharmacology when all I really want to do is thump folks on the knee and see if it springs upward. So, finding I agree with you more than I do with myself, let me turn this question on its ear: How is it, and how does it feel (if it's true), that we happen to occupy the most completely postmodernism-resistant art form, after all? I mean, I'm no David Shields, but I've made my own passing gestures at appropriation, and yet fiction—the old transaction, the old transmission—just seems to springily retake the basic shape that it was put into by Austen and Dickens (a shape only mildly deformed, in the end, by your Becketts and Barthelmes), time and time again. Because, yeah, that's what my students are writing too. I mean, compared to music (maybe) and the visual arts and film (absolutely), and even poetry, I think (assuming you're of the Ashbery-acknowledging school, as opposed to lining up in the Billy Collins-makes-me-feel-like-that-never-happened-and-I'm-relieved column).

But, but, but: You say you can read little fiction these days: Wanna tell me what you *do* think has changed?

As for Facebook, I have to admit that after all these years of believing myself a proud Luddite I have to look at the fact that I'm writing you on a computer with a wireless signal (despite having written four novels on a Selectric typewriter—I hope to stick around long enough to be the last living human who can make that claim), that I've got a cell phone (even if I don't know how to use the camera), and that yeah, I'm *sort of* on Facebook now, and just call myself a "late adopter." Yet I use Facebook weirdly, under a pseudonym, and I think I only manage to do it because I regard it as a kind of vast fiction, a tapestry-novel that we're all writing together, playing at personae (shades of Shields!). Just as I recall reading an introduction to a collection of Robert Sheckley's short stories where he confessed that the only way he could find his way into a voice for writing an introduction to a collection of stories was to pretend he was writing one more story, about a writer who's writing an introduction. And just as I've more or less solved the problem of participating in this little exchange with you by thinking of it as a story about two writers having an exchange. (They're not bad guys, these two, they just don't know what they're talking about.) My first-person voice isn't non-autobiographical, I'd never deny those overtones, but it isn't *me*, you know? I know you know.

From: David Gates
To: Jonathan Lethem
Subject: Don't follow tweeters

I'm not taking a Luddite position at all. I'm delighted to have a cell phone and wireless internet—I only wish it were faster up here in the woods. I rely heavily on Google and I waste time watching old country music clips on YouTube. (I recommend "Punish Me Tomorrow," by Carl and Pearl Butler.) It's just a matter of taste and temperament. Participating in whatever vast fiction—though Shields might think you were demeaning it calling it that—"we" might be creating sounds excruciating to me. I'm not a great fan of "we" enterprises anyway, unless they're five-piece bands with a pedal steel guitar. Nor do I want to provide information for the advertisers and marketers for whose benefit Facebook seems ultimately designed. ("A hip capitalist is a hip pig," as I used to say, back before I thought *I* could possibly be implicated.) Nor do I feel an urge to tell the world at large what I'm doing or thinking—except in some magazine, backed by advertising money, at so much a word. (Nice work if you can get it anymore.) If you're looking for bafflement on my part, here it is: I don't get why people voluntarily present themselves for online inspection. Sure, fine, okay, it's not really "themselves" they're presenting, but rather some constructed "self." Don't we do enough of that when we're offline? I don't get Twitter either. I love you like a brother—who else on God's earth would come up with the phrase "dutiful bafflement"?—but I wouldn't want to "follow" your 140-character broadcasts about this or that any more than I assume you'd want to "follow" mine, if I were to start issuing them. (Don't follow tweeters, watch the parking meters.) Many people I'm fond of are involved in this stuff; I hope they bear with what they take to be my oddness as I bear with what I take to be theirs.

But we were talking about fiction—I mean, non-vast, one-writer-one-reader fiction. I still get transported by books like, oh, Junot Díaz's novel. And maybe one or two transporting books every few years is all we ever had anyway. Part of my problem with fiction is purely personal, though hardly unique: Like a lot of writers, I review fiction and teach fiction-writing, and over the years I've come to associate reading new or unfamiliar work with professional obligation rather than with pleasure. It takes something strong now to break through my analytic coldness of heart—even in (and perhaps especially in) my own work. If I begin writing something and can see where it's going, I don't want to go there. I think that's part of Shields's objection to fiction: that he's no longer surprised, that he's impatient with the tropes he's seen a million times before. Whether the reality for which he claims to hunger is any less trite is another question.

From: Jonathan Lethem
To: David Gates
Subject: Salingerian elephants

Yeah, that *was* nice work back when we could get it, being paid to present ourselves for inspection: Advertisements for Ourselves. When there's no hierarchy in self-aggrandizement the pros fall back on silence, exile, cunning, huh? Yet I feel an old trap snapping shut, where the novelists are supposed to shut up and blunder through the dark woods like Salingerian elephants with Day-Glo targets painted on their backs, entitled only to subvocal grunting when their periodic utterances are filleted in the instantaneous opinion-marketplace. Isn't there some other version of literary practice wherein a "man of letters" would leap into this realm of commentary—at 140 characters a minute, or by whatever units of dispersal it was shoved into—without too much complaint or compromise? I've been reading G.K. Chesterton, and that mofo had something to say about each breaking info-packet as it came across his desk (newspapers published four times a day, or whatever it was), and boy was he usually both right and terrifically vivid in so doing—his "occasional" journalism still reads like breaking news. Come to think of it, so does yours, my friend, when you lower yourself to it.

But another question: So, you're Googling and YouTubing, if not Twizzling or Fnorgling, fair enough. But are your *characters* doing the same? Do you find it as difficult as I do to get this un-Brave, no-longer-that-New World onto the page in any credible way?

From: David Gates
To: Jonathan Lethem
Subject: I guess "living" is the word

I suspect you're inventing Twizzling and Fnorgling, though I wouldn't swear to it. Anyway, snow knocked the power out at my house for the past day or so, and I've been living in the eighteenth century: reading by candlelight, no running water, sending only a quick email by dial-up, from a computer running on its battery. It's a good corrective for the nostalgia I claim not to have.

No more "hierarchy in self-aggrandizement"? Well said. Yeah, I got the memo too: goodbye and good luck from the gatekeepers, upon retiring to the beach houses they presciently bought in Costa Rica. (They can have the exile and cunning; I'm fine with the silence.) Still I'm one of the lucky ones: While I could pass freely through the gate, I sneaked out enough canned goods to stock my snowy little survivalist compound.

Well, let me try to be less metaphorical. Chesterton IS ever-fresh, and I'll bet he never considered occasional journalism as "lowering" himself. Neither do I. When I did it regularly—for something like twenty-five years—I worked at it as hard as I did at fiction, and I usually found it wonderfully satisfying. It's odd how writing is writing is writing. Hell, when I read your essays, it's hard for me to imagine that your heart isn't in them as much as it is in your fiction. But do novelists NEED to be out in the "instantaneous-opinion marketplace"? I mean, it's fine with me if they WANT to. I've spent years myself clamoring to "weigh in" on the latest book by so-and-so, and if I couldn't be part of "the conversation" about such and such—that is, if Reviewer X got the gig instead of me—I felt like a wallflower. But in the long run, is there much use in con-tributing to the noise of cultural commentary? (I trust that you're not suggesting novelists respond when their OWN work is "fil-leted" in the marketplace of opinion; that's a game nobody ever wins.) There's always a new book, always a new movie, always a new record, displacing last week's new book, movie, or record, to be displaced in their turn by next week's products. And there's no shortage of commentators. Does "weighing in"—from the stand-point of one's oh-so-unique personal aesthetic, of course—help one's own work? Okay, sure, maybe, in terms of forming that aesthetic. But the constant focus on whatever new products are coming down the line can also foster a sense of one's OWN work as one more product in the marketplace—which may be accurate, but hardly helpful. Ultimately isn't it one on one—you in the room with your work, the reader in the chair with your work—with the clamor at a distance?

As to your other question, I have no idea how to handle this new mode of living (I guess "living" is the word) in fiction. I probably spend more time emailing and reading online than I do having non-virtual human contact—and I bet I'm not that unusual. If my characters were like that, would their lives be eventful enough to write about? On the other hand, if I write about people for whom the internet is—as far as the reader can see—peripheral or nonexistent, am I not essentially writing historical fiction? In the last story I finished, I used the expedient of sending my main character on a vacation where she's sworn to limit her internet and cell phone use. And how do you deal with the problem of writing something that may be dated by the time the book comes out? My novel *Preston Falls*, which appeared in 1998, has a now-hilarious account of an email exchange—"He hit Send," and so forth. And I just received a piece of student fiction which mentions Facebook and Skype in adjacent paragraphs; my instinct is that this is showing off, but maybe it's no different from Jane Austen mentioning a fortepiano and a huswife on the same page. Do you have any rules or principles or theories about this stuff—whether or not you throw them out in practice?

From: Jonathan Lethem
To: David Gates
Subject: explicit retro-stupidity

Well, let's just say I waste hardly any of my time Fnorgling anymore, after a very brief infatuation.

Rules or principles or theories—uh, no. But in fact, I did find myself wanting to explore the "virtual life" to an extent in *Chronic City*—not to weigh in with any pontifical conclusions, more just to describe the weirdness of the screens now hedging us all around, half-acknowledged. My silly solution to the problem of writing something that would "date" was akin to my approach to particle physics in *As She Climbed Across the Table* (where I made my character a resolutely obtuse humanities professor who proudly didn't "get" science): I gave my characters a dial-up modem, and burdened them with explicit retro-stupidity on the whole matter of the internet. Once they were firmly "dated," I could advance them heedlessly into the "future" that's already everyone's taken-for-granted past: eBay, for them, constitutes a mind-blowing excursion into cyberpunkery. Sort of like writing a book about characters who still think it's revolutionary to smoke hemp. Which it may be.

So, did your immersion into dial-up and candlelight—which sounds, incidentally, like the play Noël Coward might write if he'd lived to see 1996—really only correct your nostalgia? Myself, I've set up a second computer, devoid of internet, for my fiction-writing. That's to say, I took an expensive Mac and turned it back into a typewriter. (You should imagine my computer set-up guy's consternation when I insisted he drag the internet function out of the thing entirely. "I can just hide it from you," he said. "No," I told him, "I don't want to know it's in there somewhere.") In fact, you ask me whether I feel there's any difference between my fiction and essay—well, not (I ardently hope) either quality or commitment-wise (in that sense, yes, writing is writing), but lately, à la David Shields, process-wise I find I do want to Google while I essay, while I'm always certain I need that other, internet-disabled computer for writing fiction. I just finished a long essay/short book on the subject of a film—John Carpenter's *They Live*, since you ask—and though I'm proud to say I believe no one else could have written the thing (or would be likely even to have tried), and it doesn't consist either of any radical intertextuality (or borrowing or stealing), my short chapters really do launch themselves, again and again, directly out of the immediate act of reading old reviews, research, blog entries, et cetera (and the book's going to feature a lot of this stuff in the form of epigraphs, for disclosure purposes, but also the fun of it). Whereas with the fiction, despite the fact that I always admired the novel's voracious engulfment of all kinds of nonfiction modes, and of reams of research and factuality, I've suspected lately that the penetration of "information" from pretty much anywhere has suddenly become the *least* interesting move I can make. That fiction, from where I sit, now wants to go more deeply into what it alone can do—subjectivity, language, eccentric unsupported supposition, deep expressionist lying.

And—putting writing aside for a moment—wasn't it a relief to quit checking your email? I've been guessing that being offline will soon be the new luxury. Expensive safe zones in remote locales, coffee shops bragging of "No WiFi," etc. I tried to persuade Yaddo that they ought to get ahead of this curve, and reinstate a Cone of Silence approach to art colony life, but no cigar. I appear to be alone in this. They've even begun ruining airplanes, an experience redeemed only by its deep baffle of inaccessibility from the noise of connection that trails you everywhere nowadays, by installing wireless signals. (Fortunately you still have to pay, and I'm cheap.)

No, no, I won't be baited: Novelists absolutely *don't* need to be in any instantaneous-opinion marketplace; I was apparently contradicting my own beliefs there in a (useless) attempt to bait *you*. Novels and the novelists who labor over them are, essentially, elephants, steamships, space probes. Slow-moving, slow-reacting, uselessly out of touch in the reaction-time marketplace, even before its digitalized redoubling. Half the time I'm interviewed by working journalists I seem to need to spend correcting their impression that I've written a given novel out of some sudden impulsive reaction to last week's headlines, or out of feelings of rivalrous inspiration connected to other novels published a year or two before my own. Apart from the logistical impossibility of my writing anything in reaction to work I couldn't possibly have read in time—sometimes I really do feel this patronizing urge to walk them through the timeline—I just don't turn my thinking quickly enough to do it if I wanted to. The books take three or four years' thinking about before I even begin the two or three years' work (and then they sit at the publisher, fermenting, I suppose, for another nine or fifteen months). My reading's out of date; that's part of what makes it distinctive, if it is. In that sense, I suspect Hemingway was being quite honest when he talked about going into the ring with Turgenev, even if the "writing-is-fighting" paradigm seems quaintly blustery to us now. Hemingway might have simply been making the point that for a novelist, Turgenev is still *breaking news,* hot off the presses.

From: David Gates
To: Jonathan Lethem
Subject: an absolutely clean machine

Ah, News That Stays News. The old sweet song writers sang each to each in Atlantis, as the sidewalks sank and the tsunamis loomed. Still, quaint as it seems, I agree. Lots of Shakespeare's local and topical allusions are lost on us—just as yours or mine will be lost on those mutant future readers, if we're lucky enough to have any, and so what?—yet there he still is, staring straight at you.

I'm just joshing about mutants, by the way. I doubt the new technology is going to render people unrecognizable, any more than the old technologies did: moveable type, the automobile, the radio. Remember when people used to call LSD "the last fad"? Which I guess means that I don't really have to learn about a new species of human—perhaps by becoming one myself—in order to continue writing fiction. (For me, the whole woo-woo aspect of the internet, in which "reality" is always in quotes and everything's an appropriated simulacrum of an appropriated simulacrum, doesn't offer much in the way of inspiration; I've done LSD, I've read Borges.) I admit, I got worried listening to an NPR show the other day, which dealt in part with people "branding" themselves on the internet. You already HAVE a brand, it seems, whether or not you wanted one—now it's just a question of whether or not you're going to "manage" it. From this perspective, the instantaneous-opinion marketplace is only a noisy corner of a much larger marketplace, a TOTAL marketplace, in which people traffic in their very selves, or at least in the crafted images of those selves. Scary stuff, until you reflect that Chaucer, Shakespeare, and Dickens—to mention only them—knew all about it years ago. What are the Wife of Bath, Falstaff, and Mr. Micawber if not self-branders? (Or, to use Harold Bloom's much kinder phrase, "free artists of themselves.")

Still, even though I've established that the new technology's no threat to me whatsoever, I like your idea of an internet-incapable computer. Thank you. I'm going to get one of my laptops spayed immediately. I'll also need to strip out the music player and all the games (solitaire is the only one I know how to play now, but believe me, I can learn), and whatever other beguilements I'm forgetting. True, I've already got an unelectrified cabin on the top of my hill where no internet rays can reach and where I can, in theory, write for as long as my computer's battery lasts; it's just that I'm usually too scared to go up there. It might be less confusing if I brought an absolutely clean machine along. Or a yellow legal pad and a black Bic medium point.

THE OUTSKIRTS OF PROGRESS

Marco Roth

Much of your life is now spent traveling along the American Northeast, from Baltimore to Boston. Like many who've plowed back and forth along this route, you've grown overly familiar with the spectacle of ruined industry. The railroad runs past hundreds of abandoned factories; their graffiti-covered brickwork, their broken windows, the rusted hulks of machinery displayed in their weed-strewn, cracked concrete vacant lots summon a sense of an age gone missing. Gone the glovers of Newark, the machinists of North Philadelphia, the arms manufacturers of Connecticut; gone the textile mills, tanneries, and foundries. In their place have risen salvage shops, junkyards, crack dens, slag piles, the allegories of American despair. Journeys along the rail lines are like excursions into a memory of another America. They can make you feel a bit like Walter Benjamin's "angel of history," facing backwards, into the past, while blown forward by "the storm called progress," the divine wind the Japanese call "kamikaze," which heaps ruin on ruin, disaster on disaster. Except you are not moving forward, really, but back and forth, along the same tracks, past, present, and future strung in tension like all the wires, once visible above ground, now running below. One person's progress is another's downfall, an opportunity taken is an opportunity taken from something or someone else. "This door was open for you, but now I'm going to shut it," says the gatekeeper before Kafka's law.

Used, as you are, to this kind of melancholy spectacle—you're not from the cradle of civilization but the manger of industrialization—it's too easy to fall into the feeling that something, the very thing, perhaps, upon which your livelihood, your life, depends has reached some terminal stage, a crisis. You live, after all, within a matrix of "planned obsolescence." All that time you were staring out soot-smeared windows at what other people's obsolescence looked like, forces were aligning and planning to make you obsolete. You wanted to consider yourself a writer, and so you set yourself to study the writers of a past age—prose of Charles Lamb, Hazlitt, Dickens, Emerson, Thomas Carlyle, Ruskin, and Virginia Woolf—and the more recent past—Bellow, Didion, even the Beats—and the past becoming a present.

Then, one day, you forget when or who or how since it's now a pounding conventional wisdom, but maybe it was at the University of Pennsylvania, an implacably utilitarian place where you taught for a semester, someone suggested that these people mostly wrote the way they did because of the printing technologies available to them. In short, they wrote less to the dictates of their imagination or conscience than according to an invisible, iron law of technology and markets, "the industrial unconscious." There is no more history of literature, only "history of the book."

In this story's most reductive form, literary style is, in fact, nothing more than an emanation and record of the means of its delivery. The Homeric epithet arises from an oral tradition in which highly trained human memory becomes the mode of transmission; the first "novels" or Romances were an aristocratic pastime, a kind of winter parlor game for the leisured or politically outcast, so creating the heavily allegorized, digressive style of, for instance, "The Romance of the Rose," and the parody of that style in Don Quixote. This also explains the simultaneous rise of the novel in the court cultures of Europe, Japan, China, and Moghul India. The eighteenth century rise of newspapers and the serial created the multi-plot realist novel, at least in England and America, to a lesser extent; the further improvement and cheapening of the printing process led to the modernist split between the mass-produced, mass-market genre paperback and the high modernist work brought out on the cheap by irregular, small publishers.

According to this story—for it too is a story of its own time and place—the book is now reaching its end, to be replaced by the screen, whether it's a Kindle or an iPad or a laptop. Soon kids will neglect books altogether and, in a generation or two, or three, the book will seem as strange to human beings as the papyrus scroll. Libraries will shut, the grander ones turned into luxury condominiums; teenagers will stumble on the remains of the *New Directions* backlist in an abandoned warehouse, crumbling, food for worms. This change will also bring about a new writing style. People will write to the screen, as they do already: shorter sentences, quick blocky paragraphs, desperate bids to grab the reader's flickering attention, the presentation of hard facts in discrete packages with links to some external thing that imbues the writing or the writer with an aura of a more concrete "objectivity" than any mere text can now afford: e.g., "According the 2006 National Endowment for the Arts Survey, 'Reading at Risk,' literary reading is down 14 percent since 1992." Soon people may stop writing altogether, becoming curators, montage artists, tasteful arrangers, cutting and pasting and linking to the online archive of all past writing.

Even as something about this feels true to your pessimistic soul, you can't help but feel that we are not all slaves to technological progress. There are still backward parts of the world, like the theater companies of London and New York and Paris, where human beings continue to commit vast amounts of words to memory. You have friends who get drunk and recite Keats, Yeats, and Wallace Stevens. Oral culture has survived after thousands of years, and so too "book culture" will survive. We live simultaneously in several times and ages of civilization. Human beings carry the past within them as they move into the future.

The "future of the book" is, by definition, unknowable. There are only attitudes towards the future which shape possible futures from the vantage of the present: foully apocalyptic, silvery utopian, cautiously conservationist. These attitudes can even coexist within each of us. The crisis of the book is really a crisis of our free will to culture. If we commit ourselves to the culture of thought, inquiry, and rhetorical expression that arose in conjunction with the written word, inevitably we'll carry books with us in whatever shape, and inevitably we'll want to "access them" and compose them in their traditional bound and printed form, if only to feel a shimmer of connection to earlier human generations.

It's undeniable that you do want this connection and that you're not alone. American as you are, deracinated, modern, you have cause to regret so much waste, so many ruins created in the name of "fresh starts" and blank slates. The crisis of the present is a fear that the past will repeat itself, just as the psychoanalyst D.W. Winnicott suggested that the fear of having a breakdown is our way of remembering an earlier breakdown. After the buffalo were hunted to extinction on the western plains, people have belatedly tried to bring them back; along the Northeastern rail lines, the abandoned and rebuking factories have become, again, sites of interest. In part this is because we've surrendered the will and capacity to build structures like them. The knowledge they once represented is lost to us, but it did not have to turn out that way.

This is not really a book. This is a building in the shape of a book . . . a maze.

THE CRYING OF PAGE 45

Reif Larsen

Figure 1:
Erotic Technologies.

When I was still a fresh-faced young tot, I became obsessed with this curious little book called *Maze*, by Christopher Manson. You might also be familiar with it. Maybe you too spent countless hours hiding in the chicken coop with this handful of bound pages, a mere forty-five of them in all. It was not by choice, this obsession—I would have much preferred to be playing *Ghostbusters* on my friend's Commodore 64 or watching *Three's Company* or *Dirty Dancing* on our shitbox Panasonic television so as to absorb a pathological sexual tension that I craved yet still didn't understand. But both of these activities were lightly forbidden, or perhaps "heavily curtailed" would be a

Image and Epigraph from *Maze: Solve the World's Most Challenging Puzzle* by Christopher Manson. Copyright ©1985 by Christopher Manson. Reprinted by arrangement with Henry Holt and Company, LLC.

Figure 2:
The turtle is not a clue.

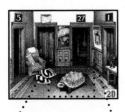

Somehow I conflated solving the riddle of the maze with adulthood. Once I found the solution, I knew I would be a grown-up. I walked around believing that all grown-ups knew the secret of this book, though I never dared ask them how they did it, for I knew they would never reveal what I would have to discover for myself. (This, I knew, was how growing up worked.)

better adjective to describe my parents' well-intentioned, pseudo-relaxed, post-hippiedom style of child-rearing, and so I was left with my crappy wooden toys and my books, and in particular, Manson's beguiling *Maze*.

On the first page of *Maze*, the reader is invited into an old, sinister labyrinth by a mysterious host who speaks in riddles and looped syntax: "Like all the others they think the Maze was made for them; actually, it is the other way around," our guide declares at the maze's entrance. Each page of the book depicts a different room of the maze in an intricate black and white woodcut, and each room has a series of numbered doors that lead to other rooms. When you choose door 20, for instance, you turn to page 20, where a new room with new doors awaits you. Such a simple, beautiful idea for a book. The rooms are laden with peculiar, often creepy clues that haunted my dreams—torn fedoras, handless statues, an abandoned cane, stuffed birds. When pieced together, the clues are supposed to eventually lead you to the glorious center of the maze, on page 45.

I never arrived at page 45. *Legitimately*, that is. I was never even sure you could actually do it, but I remember the naughty feeling of turning to page 45, breaking the thread of my path as if boring a hole through the creaky walls of the labyrinth and wondering how I could ever get there without cheating. What was amazing about this book was the powerful, unbreakable illusion it cast on my tender mind. Something about its perfect containment in a slim little book and yet its potent suggestion of this vast, three-dimensional labyrinth of silent nightmares caused me to return to its serpentine pages again and again, and in the end, with much more frequency than any quick-fix video game or illicit Patrick Swayze photoplay masterpiece.

Julio Cortázar casts a similar spell in his contranovela *Rayeula* (or "*Hopscotch*"), a wandering meditation on Paris, Buenos Aires, jazz, unrequited love, and mate-drinking, in which you as a reader are faced with a choice: read the book straight through "with a clear conscience," ignoring the last 99 "expendable chapters," or follow the directions at the end of each chapter (chapter 2 leads to chapter 116 which leads to 3 and then 84 and so on), bouncing around the book seemingly at random, until you are finally caught in an infinite loop between chapters 58 and 131. One can argue about the success of the venture, but I happen to find it heartbreaking and moving in its convolution, in its suggestion that any and all stories are possible, and in the end, no matter who is the storyteller (writer, reader, or both), all narratives fail to capture our ethereal, drifting experience on this planet. Cortázar manages to pull off these maneuvers because he never loses sight of his characters: Our anti-hero Horatio and his supporting cast of lonely urban misfits are perfectly embraced by the haphazard form and nonlinear delivery of the book itself. Then again, maybe my weakness for the *Hopscotch* experiment was simply due to a lingering nostalgia for my beloved maze, and I knew Cortázar

```
· · ·►
73 - 1 - 2 - 116 - 3 - 84
4 - 71 - 5 - 81 - 74 - 6
7 - 8 - 93 - 68 - 9 - 104
10 - 65 - 11 - 136 - 12
106 - 13 - 115 - 14
114 - 117 - 15 - 120
16 - 137 - 17 - 97 - 18
153 - 19 - 90 - 20 - 126
21 - 79 - 22 - 62 - 23
124 - 128 - 24 - 134
25 - 141 - 60 - 26 - 109
27 - 28 - 130 - 151
152 - 143 - 100 - 76
101 - 144 - 92 - 103
108 - 64 - 155 - 123
145 - 122 - 112 - 154
85 - 150 - 95 - 146 - 29
107 - 113 - 30 - 57 - 70
147 - 31 - 32 - 132 - 61
33 - 67 - 83 - 142 - 34
87 - 105 - 96 - 94 - 91
82 - 99 - 35 - 121 - 36
37 - 98 - 38 - 39 - 86
78 - 40 - 59 - 41 - 148
42 - 75 - 43 - 125 - 44
192 - 45 - 89 - 46 - 47
110 - 48 - 111 - 49
118 - 50 - 119 - 51
69 - 52 - 89 - 53 - 66
149 - 54 - 129 - 139
133 - 140 - 138 - 127
65 - 135 - 63 - 88 - 72
77 - 131 - 58 - 131 - 58
131 - 58 - 131 - 58
131 - 58 - 131 - 58 - 131 -
```

Figure 3:
The order of Chapters in
Cortazar's *Rayeula*.

was trapped in the same dilemma of pining for his own ever-elusive page 45.

I find myself again recalling the tender allure of page 45 as we stand on the precipice of reinventing the book. This sounds dramatic, and perhaps it is, for I have no doubt the book in its current printed form will endure probably as long as we manage to keep ourselves alive on this planet. There have been many announcements about the death of the printed word, about the death of the publishing industry, about the death of the novel, about the death of good literature. This is what we do whenever we sniff a change in the sea. It happened with the invention of the printing press, and the blasphemous migration of books out of the hands of the priests and into the homes of common folk; it happened with the invention of the telegraph and the perceived bastardizing of the language through abbreviation and code; it happened with the invention of the telephone and the perceived collapse of social propriety and the death of letter writing; it happened with the invention of radio and the perceived horror of a culture falling victim to lazy mispronunciation, immigrant accents, and the overall collapse of the English language; it happened with television and the perceived death of radio and the imagination; it happened with the ubiquitous growth of the internet and the mass proliferation of cell phones and iPods and robotic dogs (actually I am still terrified of robotic dogs). So fear and technology are well-acquainted bed fellows—in fact, if a new

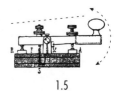

1.5

3.7

18.1

Figure 4:
Doomsday technologies

technology does not send people into a tailspin of doomsday scenarios, then chances are that this technology is not going to have any sort of pervasive cultural impact (sorry, Segway).

And yet, somehow the rise of e-books feels different than the quaint technologies I have listed above. This time, it's personal. I say this first and foremost because I am a writer and this is my domain, and so it is my turn to push the panic button and rue the loss of this brilliant technology. And yes, let us be perfectly clear: The printed book is a brilliant technology. An old technology, a relatively simple technology, but a technology that has stood the test of time. *Let us do our duty and sing the praises of books:*

1) Books are *portable*—they fit nicely in most modern handbags; we can stack at least twenty of them on our bedside table before it becomes dangerous; they can easily be lent to friends; they can be infinitely rewound without the aid of machines; you can even continue to read them during take-offs and landings.

2) Books are *palpable*—their golden ratio dimensions feel right in the lap and the hand; they smell scrumptious and unsolved when you first buy them; you can scribble notes in their margins; the turning of their pages is a metronome for the arc of our narrative processing; they get marked with the fingerprints and coffee stains of our love and neglect; you can even burn them for warmth.

THIS IS THE SMELL OF A BOOK.

3) Books are *vessels of the imagination*—they are inherently limited by their boundedness, and it is this very boundedness which gives them their great power; they allow our imagination to erect the intricate walls of the maze beyond the beautiful white margins of the page. By not showing us everything (as those uppity photoplays do), by denying us through their inherently limited evocation, books ask us to do the heavy narrative lifting, and this is why literature will always outstrip other storytelling delivery systems in terms of imaginative lasting power and the intimate, voluntary story-world participation by the reader.

For the bibliophile in all of us, this list makes us feel warm and fuzzy inside—*ah, nothing like a good book in the lap; finger and thumb poised, waiting for your eyes to catch up so that they can flip the page*—but in fifty years, this list will most likely seem ridiculous, like a Victorian-era man arguing the benefits of candlelight over Edison's newfangled electric lanterns. When I conjure how people will take their literature in the future, I see humans clutching their beloved screens or wearing their beloved Immerson-Goggles™, making gestures at a glowing, multimedia splash page that looks not unlike a three-dimensional sexed-up opening menu of a DVD.

Figure 5:
How to read a book.

"The reader" gestures to cue the ka-bling of the book trailer (which is now the new book cover), before moving cautiously into "Chapter

One," which unfortunately still demands actual reading, though is now heavily supplemented by an (optional) roving narration by "the author," pictures and music videos of the actual neighborhood the book takes place in, several risqué deleted scenes, options to improve the story on your own, and a side-panel of real-time twitter reviews. At the end of "Chapter One," the reader then makes a split-second thumbs-up/thumbs-down decision to download the rest of book or move onto the next expendable media morsel. Given this (admittedly somewhat dramatized) vision, I am both appalled and excited—for from a storyteller's point of view, the opportunities to engage a reader in new story-worlds seem simultaneously limitless and horrific.

Indeed, the voice of the storyteller appears to be the missing voice in this cacophony of press around the latest e-book reader release. The media are obsessed with examining the economics of e-books (will the Jurassic publishing industry survive?), the technology (eInk vs. LCD?), the corporate controversy (Apple vs. Amazon vs. Google!), the delicious apocalypse of the moment. But what about the actual delivery of the story? Hello: the reason we are all playing this game in the first place? The intoxication of narrative; the unsettling shiver of formal ingenuity; the silent beauty of sculptured, deeply-flawed characters; those Dada-esque metaphors which are so wrong and yet so right; those juicy, perfectly nonsensical slices of dialogue (*I can hear it! I can hear it!*)—in short,

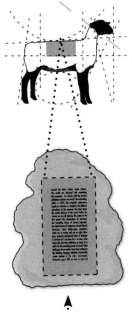

Figure 6:
Do electric sheep dream
of page design?

what about this slow-burn addiction so many of us suffer for the unending power of words? What challenges do we writers face when writing for the blinking, beeping, infinitely reframeable screen instead of the static, four-cornered, flammable page? Will we have to bend and shape our craft to the new devices or will the new devices bend and shape to us?

One starting point seems to be the persistence of the page as a delivery device. "The page" has been around in one form or another for thousands of years, and while there are some theories that the page's particular rectangular shape and orientation found its root in the natural layout of sheepskin parchment (how wonderful: Books are books because of the shape of sheep), I find it more plausible that the page's form came about the way most brilliant things come about: through slow trial and error and gradual improvement until the efficiency, design, and cost of a technology achieves optimal stool-like triangulation. And with Johannes Gensfleisch zur Laden zum Gutenberg, the perfector of movable type, we were lucky to have not just a visionary inventor but a master designer, in that he imposed a strict ratio onto his page's dimensions: the golden 5:8, which happens to nestle nicely into hand and elbow and the very skeleton of our humanness. In fact, a study by designer Jan Tschichold found that many medieval manuscripts conformed to a series of intricate ratios which he identified as the *Van de Graaf canon*. Every aspect of the page was highly purposeful, particularly the ample size of the margins, which allowed for "illuminated" illustrations to augment the manuscript, or beautiful, intricate "glosses" or commentaries to literally enfold and surround the main column of text. Tschichold, bemoaning the lost elegance of these designs, writes: "Though largely forgotten today, methods and rules upon which it is impossible to improve have been developed over centuries. To produce perfect books, these rules have to be brought back to life and applied."

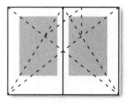

Figure 7:
The Van de Graff Canon.

When I look at these old illuminated manuscripts, I wonder at their simultaneous utility and elegance. Confronted with such considered balance, we readers secretly sigh with relief. As is the case with all of the best design, the form of the book fades into the background, allowing the content to shine through, and yet a part of us is still deeply aware that we are experiencing an object of great mindfulness, that this story will be delivered to us in the proper way, and we feel that imperceptible hum of form and content uniting in concert.

Figure 8:
A medieval law manuscript with gloss surrounding the main text.

As I write this, e-books have not been able to achieve the same sang-froid delivery hum of the book. Perhaps it is no surprise then that e-readers are currently obsessed with mimicking the printed page as best they can. The animation present in the iPad, in which you literally can watch the page turn with your fingertip, was cited as "comforting" and "satisfying" and "just like reading a real book" by early reviewers. Of course this is

Chap. 1   Chap. 2

Figure 9:
Craig Mod's fluid vertical plane,
in which the chapter becomes
the new page. These kinds of
spatial redesigns may change
the ways we think about
textual units.

nothing like reading a "real book"—whatever that means. Nor should it be. This kind of thinking is a lingering form of the "horseless carriage syndrome," in which we are trying to reconstruct old technologies in a medium that does not do old technology well. The screen cannot be fondled or written on, folded or torn. The screen does not smell (not yet, at least). We should not simply recreate the sparse beauty of the printed page on the screen. We can learn from the page's minimalism, from the power of its margins, but if we are to be true storytellers in this new medium, then we must embrace the power of the medium and move into new standards of delivery that use the page as only an instructive starting point.

Writer/designer Craig Mod, one of our most thoughtful voices investigating the future of the book, echoes my wariness of attempting to just imitate the printed book on the screen. He writes: "The canvas of the iPad must be considered in a way that acknowledge the physical boundaries of the device, while also embracing the effective limitlessness of space just beyond those edges." Mod suggests, "One simplistic reimagining of book layout would be to place chapters on the horizontal plane with content on a fluid vertical plane."

Again, when I hear this, the simultaneous excitement/horror bells go off. Content on a fluid vertical plane? But what about the tangible boundaries of my beloved page spread? What about the narrative beat of the page flip? Limitlessness of space ≠ powerful story space.

You are now probably wondering what the hell is going on in the space beneath this pop-up window and what kind of intellectual motivation I have for obscuring this text. The [...] never know what is actually beh[...] likely tearing you away from the [...] writers love this tearing, the con[...] and gentle dry-humping of our n[...] lations, where everything before [...] and our whole literary toolbox [...] glorified cardboard magic show [...] And there is much truth to this, [...] disagree, but the meta-post-mo[...] of the literary conceit cannot b[...] the line; beneath the sign and sig[...] be a bloody, beating heart. To c[...] to practice a kind of emotional [...] not interested in. Perhaps you ar[...] presume, but I think there are w[...] an awareness of the shadowbox [...] also letting it perform its discre[...] can pull off this balancing act—[...] we question its fakeness; but we love it anyway— then you are creating literature.

What used to be called the author? Excuse me? Although I can't help but be a little offended by the elimination of my job, I also can't help but be swept up in the excitement of Coover's dec- laration: It all sounds so amazing and subversive and incredibly geeky. But as I walked into my first hypertext "show" at Brown, in which students were demonstrating their hyperspace stories

---

▢▦▦▦ Choo[...]

   Maybe this is [...] as any to reveal [...] bias of mine: I ha[...] fiction. When I w[...] at Brown wall the [...] the formidable po[...] Robert Coover, a [...] of mine, the litera[...] hot and bothered [...] potential of the h[...] its capacity to blo[...] whole notion of linear narra- tive. It was exciting times. "Hy- pertext reader and writer are said to become co-learners or co-writers, as it were," wrote Coover. "Fellow-travelers in the mapping and remapping of textual (and visual, kinetic, and aural) components, not all of which are provided by what used to be called the author."

Woman physically fit, phys[...]
Physically, physically, phy[...]
Woman physically fit, phys[...]
Physically, physically, phy[...]

Woman you nice, sweet, fa[...]
Big ship on de ocean like a[...]
Woman you nice, sweet, e[...]
Big ship of de ocean like a[...]

I like to move it, move it
I like to move it, move it
I like to move it, move it
You like to move it

Monica

(several of which were just borderline cybersex choose-your-own-adventure pieces repackaged as groundbreaking post-modern electronic literature), as a "reader" of these stories, I came up against the obstacles that have, at best, prevented hypertext fiction from blossoming beyond the geekworld, and at worst, sunk the ship before it ever set sail. That is, hypertext fiction, with very few exceptions, was mostly bells and whistles, fireworks and birdcalls, virtual heavy petting and mouse clicks. These stories lacked the sense of urgency, the deep conscript of heart that traditional print narrative cultivated. Yes, there was a co-learning going on, yes the reader had become a navigator of sorts, but unlike Cortázar's *Hopscotch*, in which the inherently limited interactivity was actually raising the emotional stakes of the story, the form of these hypetext stories was dominating the content of the narrative. You were becoming a curious tapper of mouse buttons instead of an immersed, obsessive reader. If you click on this link…it shows you a naked woman. If you click on this link…it shows you a naked woman with the head of walrus. Interesting, but like most art that is produced in the world, these hypertext creations seemed to be much more engaging to create than to consume. So I left that wildly hip hypertext show at Brown and swore off the technology. *If I am going to be a writer*, I thought to myself, *then I can't get distracted with the bells and whistles. I need to learn the craft at its most bare bones.*

Figure 10:
The mouse is a condom
for the soul.

And then a funny thing happened. Eight years later, my first novel came out, *The Selected Works of T. S. Spivet*, concerning an obsessive twelve-year-old cartographer living on a ranch in Montana. And you know what? *It was essentially an exploded hypertext novel.* I had circled back around to the very thing I disdained. The key difference here appeared to be in the explosion part. In *Spivet*, all links had been expanded and mapped out on the page, and somehow the technology of the printed page really mattered in this regard—it was important to see these links laid out on a page spread, as if the reader were viewing an instruction manual of how to put together a person's mind. At the time, this formulation was a gut reaction to the needs of the character and the story, but the process of writing that book has since given me insight into my allergy to the hypertext stories of the '90s, and perhaps some useful counsel when the time comes to reach for our Immerso-Goggles™.

As writers, we are constantly battling hidden and less-hidden subtexts. The art of cultivating narrative is essentially an art of choosing what not to say and how not to say it. By allowing the reader to actively navigate these subtexts (at least those that are provided), hypertext fiction promised to dismantle the autocratic paradigm of suppression and, in a subversive, post-Freudian maneuver, invite the reader/navigator to become a collaborator of their own unconscious. The problem with this model is that while readers like the idea of control, what they really want is just a taste of this

Figure 11:
You are probably
going to die.

Just the other day a friend and I were pining away for the era of our youth. As per usual, the obsolete phenomena of Choose Your Own Adventure Books came up. "Those books always stressed me out," my friend said. "I never wanted to miss anything so I would create this elaborate system of bookmarks to trace my way back to each fork in the road. I read all 129 books in the series but I really didn't enjoy the experience. Maybe I was doing it wrong or maybe I was just afraid of dying."

control and then they want to be shown the goods. With *Spivet*, I was attempting to straddle this line between volition and orchestration—it was up to the reader to break the narrative flow by following the arrow into the subconscious arena of the margins, but in doing so, he or she also knew this disruption was scripted and somehow purposeful to a larger whole.

As Nicholas Carr points out in his book, *The Shallows: What the Internet is Doing to Our Brains*, we face a world increasingly built on the currency of disruptions—*tumblruponmydeliciousfarkdiggandtwitterallovermyfacebook*—that seems destined to rewire our brains to the point where it will be impossible for us to finish *Moby Dick* anymore. Even David Foster Wallace, the grand guru of narrative digression and recursion, declared, in his infamous Kenyon address: "'Learning how to think' really means learning how to exercise some control over how and what you think. It means being conscious and aware enough to choose what you pay attention to and to choose how you construct meaning from experience. Because if you cannot exercise this kind of choice in adult life, you will be totally hosed."

I'm not going to enact the moralist hand-wringing routine over our dwindling capacity for attentiveness (which may be our greatest asset), but given the trajectory of things, it does seem important for us fiction writers to take a step back and survey the task at hand.

For one, we are, and will continue to be, storytellers. And successful storytelling will continue to rely upon certain pillars: the slight, gnawing fishhook of suspense; the fleshing of complex, world-weary characters; the withholding (and withholding) of information; the measured lusciousness of language; the upending of expectation; the shifting of pace, mood, and scene; that counterweight loneliness of the final sentence.

Let us also not forget that despite the great movement to share all aspects of our lives via our magical devices, the actual act of reading is (and always will be) an intimate act. We read and create our story-worlds in the infinite privacy of our own mind. It is my hope that the iPad and the inevitable flood of touch-sensitive e-books may soon be able to embrace the intimacy of the act by giving us an immediate, palpable story-window that can literally be held and brushed up against. The tactility of touchscreens may finally make overlapping narratives accessible where other technologies have failed. Instead of clicking a link with a mouse, you literally touch a word, conjuring a note card that can be easily expanded, collapsed, or filed away.

This dance between form and content will continue to shift and shiver: A story about a blind woman growing up on the sea may include quiet moving images of knots and wind speed, either imbedded on the page or floating above it, and in moments where our protagonist is reading herself, Braille dots may ghost in behind the letters of the

Figure 12:
The overlap.

story, almost imperceptible to the eye. The possibilities are endless. So too are the opportunities for restraint. Indeed, knowing when to harness the power of the new media and when to let the simplicity of text work its magic may well be our greatest challenge as we continue to erect the walls of our labyrinths, searching for a solution that will never come.

NOTE ON THE COVER

Thomas Allen

When asked to come up with a cover image for this book, visions of the first home computers and cell phones—massive, unwieldy, and downright ridiculous-looking things—popped into my head! Keeping the ridiculous aspect in mind, I began work on my prototype by first affixing a mix of old type-writer and computer keys to the front cover of an actual book to reference the evolution of writing. Additional "relics" were added to continue the symbolic relationship between past and present, analog and digital: the pull-chain for backlight, the light switch for power, the ribbon spools for scrolling, the door buzzer for help, and the radio antenna for wireless access. Since e-readers blend the real (the object itself) with the virtual (the downloadable content), my version had to as well. All remaining "features" were applied digitally after the photograph was made. The only thing missing: a handsome-looking carrying case! But I'm working on it.

CONTRIBUTOR BIOGRAPHIES

Kyle Beachy is the author of *The Slide*, published in 2009 by The Dial Press. Hailed as "Suspenseful, erotic, and terribly sad," it is a ghost story, a love story, and a story of the American Midwest. He received his MFA from the School of the Art Institute of Chicago. He teaches writing and literature at the School of the Art Institute and the Graham School at the University of Chicago. His short fiction and essays have appeared most recently in *Knee-Jerk*, *Hobart*, *decomP*, and on the Featherproof *Triple Quick* iPhone application. Visit his website at www.kylebeachy.com.

John Brandon is the author of the novels *Arkansas* and *Citrus County*.

Sonya Chung is the author of the novel *Long for This World* (Scribner, 2010) and teaches fiction writing at Columbia University. Her stories, reviews, and essays have appeared in *The Threepenny Review*, *Crab Orchard Review*, *Sonora Review*, *Five Chapters*, *The Huffington Post*, and *BOMB Magazine*, among others. She is a recipient of a Pushcart Prize nomination, the Charles Johnson Fiction Award, and the Bronx Council on the Arts Writers' Fellowship and Residency. She also contributes regularly to the literary blog *The Millions*. Sonya lives in New York City and rural Pennsylvania. Visit her website at www.sonyachung.com.

Elizabeth Crane is the author of three collections of short stories, *When the Messenger is Hot, All This Heavenly Glory*, and *You Must Be This Happy to Enter*. Her work has been featured in numerous publications, anthologies, and on NPR's "Selected Shorts." She is a recipient of the Chicago Public Library 21st Century Award, and her work has been adapted for the stage by Chicago's Steppenwolf Theater Company and also for film. She currently teaches in the low-residency MFA program at University of California, Riverside. Visit her website at www.elizabethcrane.com.

Rudolph Delson was born in San Jose, California in 1975. He now lives in Brooklyn, New York. He is the author of *Maynard and Jennica*. Visit his website at www.rudolphdelson.com.

Rivka Galchen is the author of the novel *Atmospheric Disturbances*. Her writing has appeared in *The New Yorker, The Believer, Scientific American, Zoetrope, BOMB, Open City*, and *The New York Times*. She teaches creative writing at Columbia University and is currently at work on her second novel, *The Nature of Theater in Oklahoma*.

David Gates is the author of the novels *Jernigan* and *Preston Falls* and a collection of stories, *The Wonders of the Invisible World*. His fiction has appeared in *The New Yorker, Tin House, Esquire, GQ*, and *Ploughshares*. He is a former senior editor at *Newsweek*, where he wrote about books and music; other nonfiction has appeared in *The New Yorker, The New York Times Book Review, Rolling Stone, BookForum, GQ, The Oxford American, Tin House*, and *H.O.W.* He has been a Guggenheim Fellow, and his books have been finalists for the Pulitzer Prize and the National Book Critics Circle Award. He teaches at the Bennington Writing Seminars and at the MFA Writing Program at the New School.

Joshua Gaylord is the author of the novel *Hummingbirds*, a teacher of English at an elite Upper East Side prep school, and an adjunct professor at the New School. Visit his website at www.joshuagaylord .com.

Lauren Groff is the author of a novel, *The Monsters of Templeton*, and a story collection, *Delicate Edible Birds*. Her next novel, *Arcadia*, will be out in 2012. Despite being a Luddite, she has a website: www.laurengroff.com.

Garth Risk Hallberg is the author of *A Field Guide to the North American Family*. His writing has appeared in *Canteen*, *Slate*, *Glimmer Train*, and *Best New American Voices 2008*, among other publications, and has been translated into German and Spanish. He lives in Brooklyn, where he is at work on something large. Visit his website at www.garthriskhallberg.wordpress.com.

Owen King is the author of *We're All in This Together: A Novella and Stories*, and co-editor (with John McNally) of the fiction anthology *Who Can Save Us Now?* His writing has appeared in the *Bellingham Review*, *The Boston Globe*, *One Story*, *Paste Magazine*, and *Subtropics*, among other publications. He lives in New York with his wife, novelist Kelly Braffet. Visit his website at www.owen-king.com.

Benjamin Kunkel is author of the novel *Indecision* and a founding editor of the literary journal *n+1*.

Reif Larsen is the author of *The Selected Works of T.S. Spivet*. He studied at Brown University and has taught at Columbia University. He is also a filmmaker and has made documentaries in the United States, the United Kingdom, and sub-Saharan Africa. Learn more at www.tsspivet.com.

Victor LaValle is the author of the short story collection *Slapboxing with Jesus* and two novels, *The Ecstatic* and *Big Machine*. He has been the recipient of numerous awards including a Whiting Writers' Award, a United States Artists Ford Fellowship, a Guggenheim Fellowship, and the key to Southeast Queens. He was raised in Queens, New York. He can be kind of hard to reach. Visit his website at www.victorlavalle.com.

Jonathan Lethem is the author of eight novels; the most recent is *Chronic City*. He lives in California and Maine. Visit his website at www.jonathanlethem.com.

Emily St. John Mandel was born on the west coast of British Columbia, Canada. She studied dance at the School of Toronto Dance Theatre and lived briefly in Montreal before relocating to New York. She's a staff writer for *The Millions* and the author of two novels; her first book, *Last Night in Montreal*, was a June 2009 Indie Next pick and a finalist for *ForeWord Magazine*'s 2009 Book of the Year, and her second, *The Singer's Gun*, was number one on the Indie Next List for May 2010. She is married and lives in Brooklyn. Visit her website at www.emilymandel.com.

Clancy Martin is the author of *How to Sell*. He worked for many years in the fine jewelry business. He is an associate professor of philosophy at the University of Missouri. He has translated works by Friedrich Nietzsche and Søren Kierkegaard and is currently at work on a translation of Nietzsche's *Beyond Good and Evil*.

Michael Paul Mason is the author of *Head Cases: Stories of Brain Injury and Its Aftermath*. His works have appeared in several newspapers and magazines, including *Discover*, *The New York Times*, and *The Believer*. Visit his website at www.michaelpaulmason.com.

Joe Meno is a fiction writer and playwright who lives in Chicago. He is a winner of the Nelson Algren Literary Award, a Pushcart Prize, the Great Lakes Book Award, and the Society of Midland Authors Fiction Prize, as well as a finalist for the Story Prize. He is the author of five novels, *The Great Perhaps* (W.W. Norton, 2009), *The Boy Detective Fails* (Akashic, 2006), *Hairstyles of the Damned* (Akashic, 2004), *Tender as Hellfire* (St. Martin's, 1999), and *How the Hula Girl Sings* (HarperCollins, 2001). His short story collections are *Demons in the Spring* (Akashic, 2008) and *Bluebirds Used to Croon in the Choir* (TriQuarterly, 2005). He is also a professor who teaches creative writing at Columbia College Chicago. Visit his website at www.joemeno.com.

Ander Monson is the author of a host of paraphernalia including a decoder wheel, several chapbooks and limited edition letterpress collaborations, a website (www.otherelectricities.com), and five books, most recently the poetry collection *The Available World* (Sarabande, 2010) and *Vanishing Point: Not a Memoir* (Graywolf, 2010). He lives and teaches in Tucson, Arizona, where he edits the magazine *DIAGRAM* and the *New Michigan Press*. Learn more at www.otherelectricities.com.

Victoria Patterson is the author of *Drift*, which was a finalist for the California Book Award and the 2009 Story Prize. *The San Francisco Chronicle* selected *Drift* as one of the best books of 2009. Her work has appeared in various publications and journals, including the *Los Angeles Times*, *Orange Coast Magazine*, and the *Southern Review*. Her novel *This Vacant Paradise* is forthcoming from Counterpoint Press in March 2011. She lives with her family in Southern California and teaches through the UCLA Extension Writers' Program and as a Lecturer at UC Riverside. Visit her website at www.victoriapatterson.net.

Tom Piazza is the author of many book including *Why New Orleans Matters* and the novel *City of Refuge*. He writes for the HBO series *Treme*, and he lives in New Orleans. Visit his website at www.tompiazza.com.

Marco Roth is a co-founder and editor of the literary journal *n+1*. He's currently at work on a memoir about AIDS and literature, forthcoming from Farrar, Strauss and Giroux.

Nancy Jo Sales is an award-winning journalist who has written for *Vanity Fair, New York, Harper's Bazaar,* and many other publications. She has written profiles of Damien Hirst, Hugh Hefner, Russell Simmons, Tyra Banks, and Paris Hilton, among other pop cultural icons. Visit her website at www.nancyjosales.com.

Katherine Taylor is the author of the novel *Rules For Saying Goodbye*. Visit her website at www.katherinetaylor.com.

Deb Olin Unferth is the author of the story collection *Minor Robberies,* the novel *Vacation,* and the memoir *Revolution: The Year I Fell in Love and Went to Join the War.*

Thomas Allen (cover designer), who has made a career out of manipulating and photographing vintage books, lives on a 4.5-acre farm in southwest Michigan along with his gardener wife, his daughter, and an ever-expanding medley of animals. His work has appeared in numerous periodicals around the globe including *Harper's, Field and Stream, O Magazine, GQ,* and *Télérama* (Paris). He's also created cover illustrations for authors James Ellroy and Jane Hamilton. He is represented by Foley Gallery in New York and Thomas Barry Fine Arts in Minneapolis. His monograph, *Uncovered: Photographs by Thomas Allen,* was published in 2007 by Aperture Foundation.

ACKNOWLEDGMENTS

Jeff Martin

There are few things I find as rewarding as productive collaboration. This project, from concept to creation, is the result of just that. I extend my deepest gratitude to all of the authors that give this book its voice. It was a pleasure to work with each and every one of you. Thanks to Max, Denise, Anne, and of course, as always, Molly.

C. Max Magee

For your unceasing, selfless support on this and all other projects I take up, thank you Lauren. Thank you to August, for giving me something to think about and look forward to as I worked. Thank you to Jeff for your willingness to have me collaborate with you and to all of the wonderful writers who lent their time and thoughtfulness to this book. For their support, I'd also like to thank my parents, who have always fostered my literary adventures; Cara and Pat; Philip, always just a phone call away; David and Lisa; Julia and Adrien; and Greg, who chopped wood while I edited; Lucy, Steve, and Elise; Grandma Millie; and my collaborators at *The Millions*, who are always a source of energy: Garth Risk Hallberg, Edan Lepucki, Patrick Brown, Anne Yoder,

Acknowledgments

Sonya Chung, Emily St. John Mandel, Kevin Hartnett, Lydia Kiesling, Jacob Lambert, Emily Wilkinson, and Andrew Saikali. Thank you David Haglund for your great and useful suggestion and Matt Weiland for your advice. And thank you Anne Horowitz and Denise Oswald for shepherding this book to its completion.

Photo by David Miller

Jeff Martin edited the retail anthology *The Customer is Always Wrong* and in 2009 released his fabricated memoir, *My Dog Ate My Nobel Prize* (both from Soft Skull Press). He lives in Tulsa, Oklahoma, with his wife.

Photo by Lauren Karwoski-Magee

C. Max Magee created and edits *The Millions*, an online magazine offering coverage on books, arts, and culture. He lives in New Jersey with his wife and son.